Eat Britain!

"A gorgeously photographed, drool-inducing reminder of the taste of our youth... Every page made me proud to be British, and even prouder not to be French. Brown sauce, rice pudding, boiled egg and soldiers - by God, we may have lost an Empire, but we still have the greatest food on earth."

Giles Coren

Eat Britain!
101 Great British Tastes

Andrew Wheeler

Photography by Stephen Conroy
Food styling by Emma-Jane Frost
Props by Kim Sullivan
Recipes by Simon Boisseau and Andrew Wheeler

First published in Great Britain in 2007 by Friday Books
An imprint of The Friday Project Limited
83 Victoria Street, London SW1H 0HW

www.thefridayproject.co.uk
www.fridaybooks.co.uk

Text © 2007 Andrew Wheeler
Illustrations © 2007 Stephen Conroy

ISBN 13 978-1-905548-39-2

British Library Cataloguing in Publication Data
A catalogue record for this book is available from the British Library

Cover and internal design by Jason Taylor
Printed in Italy

The Publisher's policy is to use paper manufactured from sustainable sources.

To Mum and Dad – thanks for the coconut buns and crab sandwiches.

Introduction

The French can make a wonderful feast out of simple bread and cheese; the Spanish have bar food that puts most full dinners to shame; and the Italians dine like kings at every meal. Over on the Continent it is easy to eat well and take pride in your food.

In fact, whichever corner of the world you travel to, it seems that there is something wonderful to eat. Middle Eastern food has a matchless aromatic earthiness. Asian cuisine is blissfully graceful and fragrant. Latin American cooking is brimming with rustic charm and exotic spice. The world is a smorgasbord (as the Swedes would say) just waiting to be explored.

British food, by comparison, is a joke. It has a reputation for being fatty, bland and boring and the worst part is, it may be a reputation that is well deserved. However, it's not because the food itself is fundamentally bad: it's because the British don't have enough appreciation for what they've got to want to make something of it. In the countries whose cuisine we tend to celebrate, food is something that people devote their time to; recipes are passed down through generations, and the family meal is the centrepiece of the day. In Britain, dinner is all about making do, getting something down you, and having oven chips with everything.

There could be any number of highbrow sociological theories as to why we Britons have turned our backs on our own cuisine. Perhaps the Industrial Revolution lured us away from the rustic simplicity of our native pleasures? Perhaps globalisation and the British Empire gave us too many options and we lost touch with what we already had? Perhaps it was the deprivation of the Second World War that made us used to second best and parsimony? Or perhaps our laudable social progressiveness meant that neither Mum nor Dad wanted to be the one left working all day in the kitchen while the other went out to the office? It might even be that faddish fashions for olive oil and the Atkins diet have scared us away from good old-fashioned bread and butter.

It could be any of these things. It could be all of them. The only explanation that I cannot believe is that we Britons have turned our backs on British food because it isn't any good. Whatever the reason, we have become so lazy and complacent about the way we eat that our local markets are all closing down and everyone is forgetting how to cook. Anything we can't stick in a microwave, we just boil until it is grey and shapeless, and serve with too much salt.

Yet I love British food. It may be unfashionably rich and hearty, but it can also be as satisfying, indulgent and delicious as the food produced in any kitchen anywhere in the world. The only problem is convincing the rest of the world – and the rest of Britain – of this fact.

That is why I put together this list of the best of British – so that I could share my passion with people who believe that British food is nothing more than kedgeree, tripe and semolina, and convince them otherwise.

The list was originally posted to my blog so that I could share it with friends in Europe and the USA. Of course, once you stick something online, you have no idea who might read it. Soon I was getting e-mails from strangers all over the world telling me how much they had enjoyed reading about British food. Some of them were Brits showing solidarity. Some were Brits abroad, cursing me for reminding them of what they were missing. Many were non-Brits who wanted to tell me that they were now reconsidering their opinions on British food. Reading the list made people feel hungry – and what it made them hungry for was crumble, scones and bubble and squeak. I hope this book will have the same effect on you.

Before you start reading, I should warn you: this is not an objective list. I did not canvas opinions or hold a vote. It is a personal list that reflects my own idiosyncratic passions and preferences, and the only authority I can claim is over 30 years' experience as an enthusiastic eater. Now you know that this is all just my opinion, you will probably find plenty of reasons to disagree with me. There will be entries that you think are too high on the list, others you think are too low, things you don't think should be included at all, and things I have left out that you simply cannot forgive me for omitting. If that is the case, it's fine by me. I would rather people were passionate enough about British food to disagree with me than have them not care at all!

I should also add that this is an eclectic list. Most of the time the emphasis is on excellence, but nostalgic affection is sometimes an important part of why we eat. Good food should make you happy, and sometimes the best food is the kind that reminds you of childhood, or home, or holidays by the seaside. Also, some of the dishes and drinks on the list will seem inarguably and quintessentially British, while others show how Britain's historic role as a trading nation and cultural melting-pot has led to foreign influences being assimilated into a British way of eating.

You will probably notice a few recurring themes in the list as well. For example, we like to bake in Britain – it is something we are very good at – so bread and baked goods turn up throughout the list. For that matter, so do pigs. We British are unusually fond of pigs, whether it is morning, noon or night, just as long as they are served up warm on a plate, perhaps with a couple of fried eggs. We greatly enjoy our breakfasts, and just as soon as the sun is over the yardarm we enjoy a drop or two of alcohol as well. And with all those long, cold winter nights, it's no wonder that we've developed a world-beating knack for devising wonderfully stodgy puddings. All right, so the traditional British diet certainly isn't the healthiest in the world, but it is damn good for the soul.

My foodie patriotism doesn't make me blind to all the other good food the world has to offer. I will happily indulge in pungent French Brie, aromatic Thai curry, potent Mexican tequila, meaty Greek olives or big spoonfuls of American peanut butter – and these are surely all essential parts of a good, globally balanced diet.

The best of British foods deserve to be counted alongside the rest of the world's great gourmet delights, and if you don't believe me now, turn the page and I will try to convince you. With any luck, by the time you reach the end of the list, you will be as proud to Eat Britain as I am.

Haggis

Offal is a great British tradition. From tripe to kidneys to faggots, the British have always shown a great capacity for cooking up and eating the bits of an animal that other cultures are glad to throw away. It is indicative of the desperation of cold northern European cuisine. Those namby-pamby Mediterranean cultures might get to pick and choose, but we are utilitarian here in the north. We can make a memorable repast out of anything. And we will.

However, a memorable meal is not necessarily a good one, and offal definitely seems to be a tradition in decline, mourned by very few. After all, even the poorest among us today can just about do better than boiled grey cow innards for dinner. This is why we have Turkey Twizzlers, after all. (Actually, the better choice between those two might come down to a coin toss.)

Yet haggis deserves special consideration. This stuffed-stomach stomach-stuffer is a venerable thing, an icon among mystery meats, so suspect that it is actually illegal in some countries. If you've ever been served a haggis, you'll know that it is best not to think about what you are eating, because although it is now rarely made in a real stomach lining, it is still packed with all the motley peculiar bits of a beast. The beast in question is traditionally a sheep, but many haggis varieties these days are made from pigs, and when you get right down to it, does it really matter, and how would you even know?

While many offal dishes are rightly falling out of fashion,, the haggis – served with traditional 'neeps and tatties' – still makes for a fine, filling and only slightly sinister supper.

10

FOR THE RECIPE SEE PAGE 230

Wild Boar

As you read on through this list, you'll find that pig makes up a fair chunk of it – nearly 10 per cent, in fact – and for good reason. The British Isles are unusually good at producing good pig, not to mention finding good things to do with it. We may love our beef and our chicken and our lamb, but we're really a ham nation at heart. It therefore stands to reason that we would have the best wild boar in the world.

Unfortunately, there's a problem with that theory; native wild boar became extinct in Britain around 700 years ago.

Thankfully, that is not the end of the story for British boar. While repeated attempts to release boar back into the wild over the centuries generally failed because of poaching, boar farming was finally successfully reintroduced to the country in the 1980s. Wild boar is now back in Britain at last, and the dark, gamey meat of home-reared boar is available to consumers once again. The pigs come mostly from French stock, but we'll have them oinking with a cockney accent in no time.

The best news about British boar is that it is not just confined to captivity, either. There have been several escapes from private enclosures over the years, and there are now several breeding colonies of boar at large in the wild. Hopefully, they will be allowed to stick around. Wild boar belong in the British Isles, so it is good to know they are back out there – getting plump and juicy and ready to eat.

FOR THE RECIPE SEE PAGE 229

Dairylea Triangles

Somewhere beyond the realms of what we know and understand to be cheese, there exists a strange collection of substances known to the Americans as 'cheese food', or processed cheese. The best known example of this in the UK is that great lunchbox perennial, the Dairylea triangle – not to be confused with the Bermuda Triangle, which is just as mysterious but not half as peculiar. According to the ingredients, the Dairylea triangle is fully 16 per cent cheese! Yes, 16 whole per cent!

There have been a lot of strange, new cheese-inspired abominations unleashed onto our shelves in recent years, such as stringy, snack-sized blocks of processed cheese that look, feel and taste like plastic, little troughs of cheese-style mulch to gouge dry breadsticks into, and weird vacuum packs of crackers, cheese and ham that offer interactive stacking opportunities, presumably to prepare children for future employment in the same supermarkets that stock these horrors. All these freakish monstrosities are to be avoided by all sane, food-loving people.

Yet the Dairylea triangle is different. It is old school. It is a retro classic. There is an unashamed nostalgic joy in tearing the foil off one of those pale, quivering little wedges of salty, creamy loveliness. The labelling says it is a cheese spread, but it should never be spread on anything: Dairylea triangles are best served au naturel, nibbled in little lip-smacking chunks and then licked off the fingertips.

Pork Pie

Ah, the pork pie. It is both a jaunty, flat-topped felt hat favoured by jazz saxophonists, and a delightful picnic staple. Pork pie is pig all the way through – the filling is a big chunk of pork, the jelly wrapped around it is pork jelly, and even the uniquely tasty crust is made with pig fat. Pork pies are utterly piglicious.

The best and most celebrated pork pies come from the town of Melton Mowbray in Leicestershire, where they're made with an excess of plump, uncured chopped pork. So unique and iconic is the Melton Mowbray pie that its proud makers have lobbied the European Union for protected status. This would mean that only pies made in Melton Mowbray to an exact local specification would be allowed to bear the name. It would also place the Melton Mowbray pork pie on a par with such gourmet delicatessen greats as Brie de Meaux, prosciutto di Parma and Kalamata olives.

This is a lofty ambition for a humble working man's pie. After all, pork pies are the ultimate no-frills food, best served cold with a big dollop of pickle and a couple of silverskin onions. If it does get protected status, let's hope it doesn't start getting fancy ideas about being served with Sancerre and caviar.

Patum Peperium

I was introduced to Patum Peperium, or Gentleman's Relish, while idling through the food hall at one of the big upmarket London department stores a few summers ago. A lady with a tray of thinly spread pieces of toast proffered me a sample, pitching it to me as 'posh Marmite'.

It is a reasonable comparison. Patum Peperium is certainly posh, with its peculiar Latin-sounding name, gentlemanly aspirations and handsome little white pot, and, like Marmite, it is a distinctly salty spread that's best served – just as the lady at the food hall presented it – smeared ever so thinly on hot buttered toast.

However, the resemblance goes only so far. While Marmite is a thick, black, yeasty gloop, Patum Peperium is more like a grainy, greyish-brown paste; and while Marmite is made from yeast, Patum Peperium is made from anchovies – it is 60 per cent anchovy, in fact, which is quite a lot of anchovy for one spread. The exact recipe is a closely held secret that is supposedly only ever known to one person at a time, which seems like a hell of a responsibility. Presumably that person is not allowed out much.

Purists would caution against using Patum Peperium for anything other than toast, but bold iconoclasts may wish to experiment. It can be very good with scrambled eggs, for example, and it can also be stirred into meaty dishes to add a little extra savoury delight. Alternatively, you could just keep a pot in the fridge so that people think you've gone upmarket.

It is still not actually as good as Marmite, mind you.

Digestives

If the humble digestive biscuit were to be born today, some awful grinning goon in the marketing department would surely want to call it the McVitie's Wheatie Dunkable.

Dunking, you see, is what this king of biscuits is for. It has the ideal density and absorbency for a quick dip in a lovely hot mug of tea, and its warm mealy flavour is the perfect compliment to a cuppa. What could be more satisfying than having that tea-sodden wheaten biscuit dissolve into mush in your mouth?

In some circles it is considered ill-mannered to dunk, which just goes to show that good manners owe nothing to good sense. If we are not allowed to dunk our biscuits in our tea, we might as well not bother getting up in the morning.

Of course, if it had been called the Dunkable, we would all be well used to the name by now, since the odd name 'digestive' barely raises an eyebrow any more. In fact, the digestive already owes its name to a peculiar marketing notion; it was invented in 1839 by Alexander Grant, who believed that the inclusion of bicarbonate of soda in the recipe would make his new biscuit a perfect aid to digestion.

If it genuinely had any such health-giving properties, I'm sure we'd hear no end of it today. Yet, whatever their effects on the body, digestives are certainly good for the soul. The digestive is a dependably homely sort of biscuit.

Hotpot

The fine art of cookery probably started with a stew. One glorious day back in the distant mists of time primitive cooks went out into the fields in search of an animal to tear a chunk off, and a few roots that they were pretty sure were not poisonous. Then they threw everything in a pot and left it to bubble away over the fire for most of a day, and the result was a lovely hearty stew.

Stew is really a fundamental culinary concept, and wherever you go in the world there's some wonderful indigenous variation. In the Americas they put a bit of a kick in it and it became chilli. In India they stirred in some fragrant spices and transformed it into curry. In Hungary they added paprika and suddenly it was goulash. And in France they added a waft of snooty disdain and it became cassoulet. There's nothing fancy or inventive about throwing everything in a pot – but no one ever said that good food had to be fancy.

Somehow Lancashire has managed to lay claim to the best-known British version of the one-pot stew, which traditionally involves lamb and potatoes. One suspects that the people of Yorkshire might have been able to come up with the idea as well, but the Lancastrians were first to the patent office. Still, regardless of where it is made, hotpot is as solid and satisfying a meal as you're likely to encounter.

FOR THE RECIPE SEE PAGE 228

Butterscotch

The culinary history of boiled sugar is complicated and enigmatic. It seems that toffee was most likely invented by the Americans – though they call it taffy – and caramel must surely be credited to the French. The British, however, can definitely lay full claim to butterscotch, the deliciously creamy vanilla sweet that has also become a classic kitsch flavouring. The name seems to suggest a Scottish inventor, but the credit actually belongs to Doncastrian candyman Samuel Parkinson, with 'scotch' being a corruption of 'scorch': butterscotch is essentially scorched butter.

Beyond the well-known sweets, butterscotch is also available as a rich, deadly sauce, or as a particularly sickly schnapps. And then there's the form in which most of us probably discovered it for the first time. It comes as powder in a packet. You add milk and it turns into paste. Then you stick it in the fridge and it turns into pudding.

Yes, it is Angel Delight, a super-sweet and sloppy dessert, and a children's favourite for generations. Objectively speaking, it is sort of revolting – yet every once in a while I get that creeping urge to stick a spoon in a gelatinous glob of wallpaper-beige milky butterscotch-flavoured pudding, and I can rarely resist the temptation.

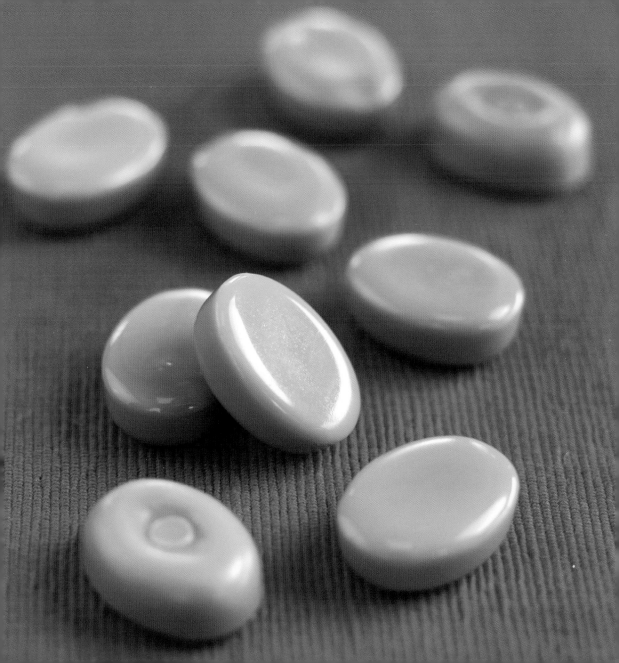

Parsnips

It was a sad day for the humble and hard-working parsnip when, in the late sixteenth century, the potato found its way from the New World back to Europe. Although it took another couple of centuries for the potato to really catch on, the arrival of the Johnny-come-lately tuber was always going to be bad news for the parsnip. Parsnips were once Britain's root vegetable of choice, uniquely suited to the climate because their flavour is enhanced by frost, but now Britain is undeniably a potato-loving nation.

Perhaps it is time for a parsnip revival. Parsnips still have a lot to recommend them, after all. They're healthy, filling and remarkably nutritious; they're packed with sweet, nutty flavour; and they're sturdy little winter survivors. In fact, the transatlantic tuber travel was not just one way – the first visitors to the New World took the parsnip across with them, and could well have all died out without the robust root to feed them.

However, parsnips are not very popular in America today – they're actually regarded as a weed over there – and they're not a great deal more popular in Europe either, perhaps because they lack the potato's versatility and can develop a tough, woody core if they're left sitting around too long. Once you've learnt how to handle parsnips, however, there's a lot that can be done with them. For example, roast parsnips with a sweet honey glaze are an excellent accompaniment to any Sunday lunch, and curried parsnip makes for a first-rate winter soup.

Scampi

Scampi in its native form is known by many names – and none of them sound the least bit British. It is called the Norway lobster or the Dublin Bay prawn, though it is technically neither a lobster nor a prawn. If you want to get terribly posh about it, you can call it by its French name, the langoustine. Even the word 'scampi' itself is not English – it is Italian.

So what makes it a great British meal? Well, first of all it is fished in our waters, which we just happen to share with the Irish, French and Norwegians. Second, we're the ones who deep-fry our 'Norwegian lobster' tails in batter and serve them up with a wedge of lemon, and that's scampi at its best.

Scampi has picked up a bit of a bad reputation in the UK – a reputation a million miles away from anything that might appear on a menu as langoustine. If you're ordering scampi these days, you're probably either in a pub or at a dog track, and what you'll get served will be greasy little lumps of suspect random prawn in a basket, often on a bed of soggy chips.

Real scampi is exactly as good as something calling itself a langoustine should be – fat, succulent, pink, meaty mouthfuls, wrapped in a toasty crust and doused with a spray of sharp, fresh lemon juice.

FOR THE RECIPE SEE PAGE 228

Teacake

What is a teacake? This is a question that has plagued scholars and philosophers for centuries, especially in the north of England. Is it a type of chocolate-covered marshmallow with a biscuit base? Is it a fat little puck of desiccated coconut? Is it a rather boring plain bread bap?

Of course, it is none of these things, though they have all tried to claim the name, and they all have their place in the world – especially the chocolate-covered marshmallow, which the good people at Tunnock's still insist on calling a teacake for reasons known only to them.

A teacake is in fact a sweet currant bun, served toasted and buttered with a big mug of tea. Some people like to add a bit of jam, but I think the melted salty butter smothered over hot juicy raisins and currants tastes sweet and delicious enough as it is.

It is worth noting that the British have a particularly pronounced love of bread, as this list will show at some length. We eat bread with breakfast, lunch and dinner, as well as at teatime and for dessert. We even put dried fruit in it and claim it is a type of cake. Not that I'm complaining.

King Edward Potato

All right, so the potato is a foreign invader, an upstart *arriviste* that has shouldered out our native parsnip as the number one root. Still, there's no reason why parsnips and potatoes can't live together in harmony, and the potato is surely now too important a part of the British diet to be idly dismissed. You can't make a hotpot without it, or, for that matter, fish and chips, bubble and squeak or a chip butty.

To my mind, the most British thing you can do with a potato is roast it, and the ultimate roast potato is surely that most monarchical of spuds, the noble King Edward. A few floury, aromatic King Edwards, par-boiled and roasted in plenty of sizzling hot goose or beef fat, make the ideal accompaniment to Sunday lunch – crisp and golden on the outside, steaming and fluffy on the inside. They also make excellent jacket potatoes to enjoy with the fireworks on Bonfire Night, and they're the perfect base for a thick, warming soup.

Potatoes may not originally be British, but the King Edward certainly is. It was first cultivated in Northumberland in 1902 – a cross of the Magnum Bonum and Beauty of Hebron potato varieties. It was originally named Fellside Hero, but was patriotically rebranded in the wake of the Second World War in honour of King Edward VII, who bore more than a passing resemblance to a potato himself.

Piccalilli

There are some foods that the whole world catches on to, such as tomato ketchup or chocolate, and then there are foods at the other end of the scale, that never quite seem to find their place in world cuisine, and sometimes are not even fully trusted back home.

Piccalilli definitely belongs in the latter category. It is lumpy, pungent and tart, and has a colour that puts one in mind of radioactive waste. To be blunt, it is funny-looking food. I will go further and say that it simply looks wrong. Generally speaking, one should avoid putting anything in one's mouth that is both yellow and chunky unless it's cheese and pineapple on a cocktail stick. So piccalilli is a difficult beast. You really have to understand it in order to give it the love it so richly deserves.

Of course, my patriotic pride demands that I both understand and love piccalilli. Piccalilli is what happens when two areas of peculiarly British culinary interest collide – pickling and currying. This spicy pickle is full of elements that the British palate first introduced to each other, as the constituent vegetables – cauliflower, gherkins, onions and others – are steeped in a vinegary sauce seasoned with mustard, turmeric and ginger. The result is a vibrant, crunchy mixture of bright yellow brilliance that is quite unlike anything else you'll ever put on your plate, but in the best possible sense.

Irn Bru

The fizzy drink is not a British speciality. While the practice of carbonating water was first perfected by an Englishman, Dr Joseph Priestley (better known for his work on the discovery of oxygen), it was our cousins in the colonies who came up with the idea of selling this refreshing 'health drink' with added herbal flavourings, such as dandelion and sarsaparilla. Root beer, cola and an infinite variety of other sugary soda drinks soon followed.

Still, not all fizzy drinks hail from North America. No, just the successful ones. While Coca-Cola and Pepsi Cola share dominion over the world's soft drink industry, we here in Britain have tried to shoulder our way in for a share of the action.

The result has been such wannabe medicinal delights as the mysteriously 'red-flavoured' Tizer ('the appetizer') and Manchester's grape, blackcurrant and raspberry drink Vimto ('vim tonic'). The best of the lot, though, is Scotland's dazzlingly orange Irn Bru, which boasts a flavour that can best be described as 'Irn Bru'. Rather impressively, Irn Bru remains locked in a tussle with Coca-Cola for market supremacy in Scotland; it is one of the few drinks in the world that can take on Coke, even if only in its own back yard.

Irn Bru is allegedly made from girders, but science informs us that it contains only 0.002 per cent ammonium ferric citrate, which, sadly, is not even enough to make a paper clip.

Christmas Pudding

Christmas, as we know, is all about food.

All right, there's a little bit more to it than that – there's a lot of drinking to be done, for example, and there are the presents of course, and there are usually some rows to be had and a good whinge about how there's nothing good on television. However, the main point of Christmas is food, and every December we get free rein to enjoy a whole host of treats that we never get to see during the rest of the year, including mince pies, brandy butter, cranberry sauce, sprouts, eggnog and mulled wine. But the best and most British Christmas treat is Christmas pudding.

As it happens, at my family Christmases we're completely stuffed by the time we're finished with the main course, and there's not really any room for pudding. We light the blue brandy corona half-heartedly and hack a few chunks out of the pudding's glistening black dome. Then we roll nuts and raisins around on our plate to make swirls in the brandy butter while the turkey and stuffing sit heavy in our stomachs and we try to summon the energy to stagger to the sofa.

This ought to be a tragedy, but, on the contrary, it is actually a wonderful thing. You see, the best way to eat Christmas pudding is not on Christmas Day at all. In an ideal world you will be left with a surfeit of pudding on Boxing Day, and then you can dip it in brown sugar, fry it in butter and serve it for breakfast with a glass of champagne. That, to me, is the best part of Christmas. Happy birthday, Jesus!

Cucumber Sandwiches

Modern vicars are clearly a lazy and feckless lot, as I cannot remember a single occasion on which my local vicar has popped in for tea. In fact, I don't even know who my local vicar is. Come to think of it, I'm not entirely sure where the nearest church is. Clearly, my vicar is failing completely in his duties. As a direct consequence of his lack of social conscience, I am starved of opportunities to enjoy cucumber sandwiches. Chances are my soul is on patchy ground as well.

It is probably too late for my soul, but I shall have to find other excuses to make the sandwiches, as I'm now resigned to never seeing the vicar, and I do so enjoy a good cucumber sandwich.

As sandwiches go, the cucumber variety is a bit of a peculiarity – it is not particularly flavoursome, and it is certainly not nutritious. It is a fussy aristocratic indulgence of the first order. Yet, like a long, tall glass of water on a warm summer's day, it has amazing restorative powers. Its simple, fresh flavour is a cleanser for the palate and the mind.

There's nothing fancy in its wondrous alchemy – no cream cheese or salmon or pickles – it is just cucumber, fresh bread, butter and salt. And that's all you need. Should my vicar ever wish to join me for cucumber sandwiches, all he needs to do is call and we'll see if we can arrange something. Although, now I come to think of it, I'm Catholic, so maybe that's why he never comes around.

FOR THE RECIPE SEE PAGE 228

Apple Sauce

When it comes to sauce there is just one great nation that stands head and shoulders above all others, and that can proudly proclaim itself as the master sauce-making nation.

Unfortunately for us, that nation is France. Yes, I admit it, the French are the world's great sauce innovators, with culinary accomplishments that include mayonnaise, hollandaise, béchamel, Béarnaise and beurre blanc. They probably have more varieties of sauce per head than they have bars of soap. Still, they can't entirely turn up their noses at the British, because we have a few good sauces of our own, and this is only the first of them to make the list.

It was ultimately necessary for the British to invent apple sauce because of our pronounced fondness for pork: there are few flavours that make for a better marriage than pork and apple. A chunky bowl of glistening sweet and sharp apple sauce is an unbeatable accompaniment to roast pork, gammon or even some lovely fat bangers. I'm told that apple sauce is also good for babies, but on the whole I'd rather have it on pork.

FOR THE RECIPE SEE PAGE 227

Scotch Egg

Like the pork pie, the Scotch egg is one of the great picnic foods. You can always tell a good picnic food because it fits in your hand, you can eat it without utensils and nothing gets thrown away.

The Scotch egg is also one of those foods that don't have a very good reputation these days, and that's because the ones you'll find on most supermarket shelves simply are not up to scratch. The eggs are like rubber, the meat tastes of cardboard, and the whole thing dries up your mouth, leaving you feeling as if you have just gargled with chemical preservative.

There's no reason why it has to be this way. Take the Scotch egg back to basics and you can see that it is a winning concept; it is a hard-boiled egg wrapped in sausagemeat and fried in breadcrumbs. It is sausage and egg, for goodness sake! Surely that ought to be a glorious treat for any self-respecting food-lover? And so it is, if you're prepared to go hunting for the good stuff.

One place that knows a good egg when it sees it is that epicurean paradise, the Fortnum & Mason food hall. In fact, anyone who thinks that the Scotch egg is a working-class hero among foods may be surprised to learn that it was not invented by some bristling Highland sheep herder in a kilt. The Scotch egg was actually invented at Fortnum & Mason back in 1738, and has been sold there ever since.

Queen of Puddings

When it comes to compiling a celebratory list of British foods, it would probably be a simple thing just to draw up a list of puddings and be done with it. We Britons have a particular affection for 'afters'. As a nation we have probably spent more time devising new ideas for using sponge, butter and cream than we have on any other culinary exertion. We probably have more hot puddings than we have hot dinners.

For propriety's sake I'm limiting myself to a mere handful of desserts in this list because I believe we've got so much more to be proud of than just great puddings. Unfortunately, this means that there's no room for such school dinner classics as spotted dick, summer pudding and jam roly-poly. In fact, in a move that may horrify many, I'm giving over their place on the list to a pudding of relative obscurity.

Queen of puddings consists of a breadcrumb-based egg custard and a frothy whipped meringue separated by a thin Maginot Line of bubbling red jam, and it has three major advantages that have earned it a special place in my affections.

First of all, it represents three of the great pudding families: the hot jam family, the custard family and that foreign pretender, the meringue family. Second, it has a royal pedigree. According to urban legend, it was devised in the kitchens of Buckingham Palace for miserable monarch Queen Victoria herself. This is probably not true, but it certainly sounds good. Third, it really is an excellent pudding, albeit one that should probably be enjoyed sparingly. When you get right down to it, queen of puddings is three doses of cooked sugar stacked one on top of the other. It is ridiculously sweet, but ridiculously good.

FOR THE RECIPE SEE PAGE 227

Leeks

Phoenicia: an ancient maritime civilisation spanning the Mediterranean from around 1200 to 900 BC. Its many notable achievements include the establishment of a massive mercantile empire, the spread of an alphabet that became our own, and the introduction of the leek to Wales.

Yes, one of Wales' great national symbols is a foreigner. Actually, two of them are – the daffodil also came from the Mediterranean. Mind you, at least St David was a real native, which is more than can be said for saints Andrew, Patrick or George.

Legend has it that it was during a fight against invading Saxons that the Welsh first pinned leeks to their hats so that they could distinguish themselves from the outsiders. Evidently, they have been eating them ever since. Leeks, that is. The Welsh gave up eating outsiders in the late nineteenth century.

Leeks are often regarded as a poor man's vegetable, but they deserve to be held in much higher esteem. They're part of the noble Allium family, along with onion and garlic, which means they offer many of the same health benefits, such as boosting the immune system and helping the heart. They also boast a more graceful but no less distinctive flavour. Leeks are great in a soup or raw in a salad, but the best way to serve them is the way my dear Welsh mother always did: boiled, wrapped in ham, and baked in a thick, rich cheese sauce.

Double Gloucester

'Three hurt in cheese rolling race' – so read a BBC news headline in 2005, describing what one presumes was a gentle, whimsical sort of mayhem at the annual cheese rolling event at Cooper's Hill in Gloucestershire.

In fact, it seems that a few bumps and bruises are an unavoidable feature of the festivities at Cooper's Hill, where every year the locals run full pelt down a steep hill in pursuit of a rolling Double Gloucester that's hurtling away at up to 70 miles per hour. Quite why they engage in this potentially suicidal sport is not entirely clear, except that the good people of Cooper's Hill claim that they've been doing it for centuries, possibly as far back as Roman times. Well, it gets them out of the house, I suppose.

The 'double' of the cheese's name arises from the fact that it is made from a double yield of Old Gloucester cattle milk – the first and last yields of the day – making it an especially rich, buttery cheese. There has been some concern that Double Gloucester might not have much of a future, though, as in the 1970s the Old Gloucesters were reduced to just a single herd.

Thankfully, specialist breeders have since been fighting to bring the breed back from the brink of extinction, so with any luck Double Gloucester is not going to end up on the endangered species list any time soon. After all, it is clearly a cheese worth risking your neck for.

Bread and Butter Pudding

Let's be blunt here; low-carb dieting is a thoroughly unBritish practice. A parliamentary committee should be convened, and special enquiries should be made, and people refusing to support the baking industry should be placed on some sort of blacklist and refused the vote. They should be asked, 'Are you now, or have you ever been, on Atkins?' Breadlessness is simply not proper behaviour.

Of course, every good witch-hunt needs its version of a ducking stool. For this special inquiry the test can be bread and butter pudding. Everyone gets a serving, and anyone who doesn't ask for seconds is suspect.

The great joy of bread and butter lies in its versatility, and it is more than capable of integrating a bit of foreign influence or some fancy-pants extra ingredients without losing its essential British character. Croissants, brioche or panettone can all make an excellent base for the pudding, and variations can include raspberries, chocolate, ginger, marmalade, peanut butter or whisky.

Whatever the ingredients, the secret of good bread and butter pudding is in the soak. The buttered bread needs to be saturated in a wonderful soup of milk, cream and butter that's been seasoned with nutmeg, cinnamon and sugar. Every grandmother probably has her own perfect formula, and if yours doesn't, she's probably a witch.

FOR THE RECIPE SEE PAGE 226

Fried Slice

Another meal, another slice of bread. In France when they fry up bread for breakfast it is a swanky affair, something like a one-man bread and butter pudding. They submerge the bread in a bowl of spiced beaten egg, then they serve it with cream or jam or just a frosting of sugar. There's no denying that it is really a rather wonderful thing.

But we have our own back-to-basics version of French toast in Britain, and there's nothing snooty about a fried slice – it is just bread, fried. Nothing could be easier; neither could it be much deadlier. Fried slice is a particularly dangerous breakfast sin, and it doesn't really have a single morally redeeming feature. It is bad bread – usually nutritionally void supermarket white sliced – and it is doused in bad fat – vegetable oil or butter, or the bubbling meaty juices from your morning sausage or bacon. It is awful, terrible, dreadful stuff.

Yet, of course, it is wonderful. It is a glorious golden indulgence – crunchy and crisp at the edges and deliciously greasy in the middle – perfect with a fried breakfast and wonderful with a hot cup of tea. For those days when a slice of toast just won't do, you should treat yourself to a fried slice. Just don't treat yourself too often.

FOR THE RECIPE SEE PAGE 226

The '99' Cone

What did Margaret Thatcher ever do for us? She didn't even make the trains run on time! But she did make one crucial contribution to British culture: back when she was a chemist, she helped devise the chemical process behind whipped ice cream. It seems like a generous act until you realise that this was a cunning way to make a little ice cream go a lot further by pumping it full of air.

It is probably a bit of a stretch to say that the stuff in a '99' cone is ice cream at all, as it is mostly vegetable oil and sugar. Still, it would surely be the height of foolishness to be puritanical about anything served out of the side of van, and that puffy white swirl of glistening creamy ooze, served in a biscuit cone and stabbed with the all-important Cadbury's flake, really is one of the great joys in life. Getting sticky-fingered as the ice cream melts down onto the cone is the stuff that childhood summer holidays are made of, and every child devises his or her own methodology for attacking the '99'. Personally, I liked to push the flake down inside the cone, then pack the ice cream in around it with my tongue so that eating the cone was like enjoying a little chocolate and ice cream sandwich.

Some ice cream vans these days like to visit office car parks, tinkling their little jingles to summon the wage slaves outside for a summer treat – and that music triggers a strange Pavlovian response in otherwise responsible adults, luring them outside to relive their childhood summers with a little taste of Thatcher's Britain.

Chelsea Bun

When I used to enjoy Chelsea buns as a child, unravelling the sweet doughy curls and washing them down with a big glass of milk, I would like to imagine that Chelsea was a rather sweet, cosy place, where children played with a hoop and stick on the cobbled streets, and washing hung out on the line. Much like the town of Bakewell, probably.

Anyone who has ever been to Chelsea knows that it is nothing like that, and its inhabitants are most certainly not the sort of people you would expect to see scoffing sticky buns. In fact, I expect little Jonquil is allergic to yeast, while Araminta can't be made to eat anything with currants in it, and anyway, Chelsea buns are simply not organic. In fact, rather revealingly, there are no Greggs bakeries anywhere in Chelsea, so if a yummy mummy had a sudden craving for cake, she would have to drive her absurd suburban tractor to Battersea, perhaps stopping off on the way back from pilates.

Mind you, as it turns out, the Chelsea bun is not strictly from Chelsea at all. It was first baked in the eighteenth century at the Chelsea Bun House in neighbouring Pimlico. Still, that's close enough.

Far from being disdained by high society, the first Chelsea buns were hugely popular with King George II and III – the German one and the mad one – and such royal endorsement ensured that they became a hit with the population at large. And quite right, too; who wouldn't enjoy that gooey, rich, sticky swirl of dough spiced with cinnamon, stuffed with dried fruit and topped with a sugar glaze? Apart from poor Jonquil, of course.

Gooseberries

You would be forgiven for thinking that nothing good grows in Britain, if for no better reason than we can't seem to produce a decent variety of grape. Most great culinary nations would be deeply ashamed to admit that they cannot make a decent bottle of wine. We should be more ashamed that we keep trying.

The simple truth is that fruit knows where it wants to grow, and it is not easily fooled. Grapes don't want to be here, and they're going to be very resentful if we keep trying to grow them. Meanwhile, there are other fruits that thrive in our climate, and they're not getting anywhere near as much love as they deserve.

High up on that list of neglected local treasures is the gooseberry. It is not the prettiest-looking fruit in the world, given that it resembles a hairy alien egg sac from a sci-fi horror movie, but it has a wonderful flavour that is unique. Gooseberries have a lip-puckering juicy sourness that makes them perfect in puddings, pies and jams, and they are the ideal accompaniment to gamey meats. Gooseberries probably derive their name from the French word for them, *groseilles*, rather than from any association with geese, but many chefs say that goose and gooseberry do make an excellent combination.

Bubble and Squeak

Leftovers deserve much better than the compost heap, and the ability to turn yesterday's remains into today's dinner is what sets a good cook apart. In Britain the ultimate test is the eccentrically named bubble and squeak.

What makes bubble and squeak special is that it is not just any old leftovers; it is leftovers from the Sunday roast. The potatoes get smashed and thrown in a pan, then the cabbage and sprouts and any other leftover veg are tossed in, and the whole thing is fried until golden brown. If you're feeling particularly bold, you can throw in the leftover meat as well, as was once traditional. In theory the whole glorious concoction should bubble and squeak in the pan, hence the name, but if it doesn't, don't feel compelled to do the bubbling and squeaking yourself.

As Sunday roasts and family lunches have tended to fall out of fashion, bubble and squeak has also become less common. There's no reason that bubble and squeak has to be made from leftovers, of course: one can make a perfectly good bubble and squeak from freshly boiled potatoes and greens, though it will never taste quite the same.

Bubble and Squeak are also the names that a lot of people give to their first pets, or so I like to believe. It is what I called my hamsters.

FOR THE RECIPE SEE PAGE 226

Caerphilly

Legend has it that Caerphilly cheese was popularised by the coal miners of South Wales. They would be working so hard down in the dark and dust that they would sweat out all their bodies' essential minerals, leaving them with a desperate craving for salt. As there were no fancy shower gels in the mines to replenish them, they would take whole cakes of Caerphilly down to the coalface and munch away on them throughout the day.

If the story is true, it makes me envious of a life in the mines. All right, it was probably oppressive and exhausting and life-threatening, but what a great excuse to eat huge blocks of cheese!

Even if the story is not true, Caerphilly is undoubtedly a delicious cheese – creamy, crumbly and tangy, and perfect for eating just as it comes. It is also a particularly good cooking cheese, or a welcome addition to salads or sandwiches. Caerphilly gets its salty flavour from being bathed in brine and, unlike many British cheeses, it is at its best when it is fresh, rather than matured. For that reason, mass-produced Caerphilly is generally not very good, so to get a real sense of how wonderful this cheese can be, seek out a small-batch, traditionally made, unpasteurised variety. Then eat it in a cave.

Parkin

Ginger is about as non-native as British food gets. It hails from southern China, but found its way across Asia and Africa and all the way to the Caribbean, establishing itself en route as one of the culinary greats, popular in every cuisine.

Somehow it even found its way to this cold, wet, blustery cluster of islands set in a frozen sea in the north of Europe, and its exotic heat and volatile pungency found a receptive audience. We don't grow ginger over here – we're not nearly tropical enough – but we do seem to like eating it. We have baked it into gingerbread men, ginger snaps and ginger nuts, and we have incorporated it into our sweets and drinks, including ginger creams, ginger fudge and ginger beer. We are slaves to ginger.

Ginger also crops up in one of the most highly prized cakes in the great British tea-room: Yorkshire parkin. This fine, comforting, cloying loaf cake is traditionally associated with Bonfire Night, when a little warmth and spice helps to keep a person going while standing out in the wind and rain to watch the fireworks. It is also very good warmed up and served with custard or a thick dollop of butter.

Ribena

In wartime we are told that it behoves us all to do our duty, and apparently this extends down to even the lowliest little purple berry.

Blackcurrant syrup was first developed in 1933, and it was discovered to be an excellent source of vitamin C. It did not take on the brand name Ribena (from *Ribes negrum*, the Latin for 'blackcurrant') until the late 1930s, at which point it was sold to hospitals and maternity wards, essentially as a health-giving vitamin supplement. When the Second World War came and Britain was cut off from its orange supplies, Ribena was put on the ration books as source of vitamin C for children. In our time of great national need, Ribena was there to save a whole generation from the curse of scurvy. It probably did not do their teeth much good, though, as Ribena has more sugar in it than Coca-Cola.

To this day, Ribena is a drink that many people associate with health. Like Lucozade, it is a drink to enjoy when you are knocked out by the flu, and need plenty of fluids and a good dose of vitamin C. It can also be diluted with hot water, making it a wonderful syrupy salve for a sore throat.

However, Ribena is not just there for the bad times, like war and plague. In moderation, it is a fabulously fruity treat at the best of times as well. If you're really strange, you can mix it with cider and beer to make the traditional Goth favourite Snakebite and Black, though drinking that stuff is its own special kind of sickness.

Cornish Pasty

It may surprise you to hear this, but this hearty baked savoury pastry pocket, stuffed with chunks of meat and seasoned vegetables, is actually good for your health, but only if you're at particular risk from cave-ins. Bear with me and I will explain.

Cornish pasties famously owe their origins to tin mining, when they were devised as a way of wrapping up a filling lunch in one easy-to-handle package for men who were not going to see sunlight all day. What made pasties particularly perfect for the job is that they are extremely filling and full of energy, and they can stay warm for hours.

Legend has it that early pasties were savoury at one end and sweet at the other, but there is no real evidence to suggest that this is true. A more appealing legend is the one about cave-ins. It is said that the women who baked the pasties would etch their husbands' initials into the thick, crimped crust. The miners would then hold the crust to eat the pasty, thus covering the crust in muck and making it inedible. The crusts would be thrown away as an offering to the knockers (the spirits who live in the mines) and the man whose initials were carved into the crust would thus be saved from the knockers' mischief for that day. In this way he was apparently safe from cave-ins.

Cornish pasties are an eminently British speciality, but there was a time (during the nineteenth century) when the skills of Cornish tin miners were in high demand across the globe, and wherever they went, from America to Australia, they took their love of pasties with them. To this day, many little towns around the world that developed from mining communities still produce pasties of their own.

FOR THE RECIPE SEE PAGE 225

Wild Scottish Smoked Salmon

As a general rule, you are better off eating Pacific salmon than the Atlantic variety. Pacific salmon is more likely to be wild – and therefore tastier – and is less likely to be full of pollutants – and therefore healthier.

However, good wild Atlantic salmon is still out there, and though it costs a pretty penny, it is worth the price. The everyday salmon that you might enjoy in a prepackaged sandwich or a box of Westernised sushi is perfectly fine for the working week, but when it comes to high days and holy days, wild Scottish smoked salmon is a class apart. In fact, wild Scottish salmon is a serious delicacy, with a delicate yet distinctive smoky flavour and a meltingly soft meaty texture.

A taste like that should never be wasted, so if you're going to indulge in some top-notch salmon, try not to eat it with too many competing flavours. It is certainly not for smothering in sauce or putting in a pie. To enjoy it at its best, serve it on generously buttered slabs of malted wholemeal bread with a little salt and pepper and a squeeze of fresh lemon juice, and perhaps a glass or two of champagne.

FOR THE RECIPE SEE PAGE 225

Jaffa Cakes

Even as I type this, I am enjoying a Jaffa cake – and according to the packaging, they're recommended by sports nutritionists... perhaps as a sort of small Frisbee?

It is a sad state of affairs when we have to try passing off our epicurean treats as health foods. People don't really get fat from eating Jaffa cakes; they get fat from eating chips with every meal and spending all day sitting in front of the TV. If you are unhealthy, it is because you are not exercising enough and your diet is not balanced. The presence of a couple of Jaffa cakes next to your tea at three o'clock in the afternoon is not the thing that is going to make the difference. We should not be so ashamed of our little indulgences that we have to fool ourselves into thinking that these small, chocolate-topped sponges with their smashing orangey bits are some sort of giant brown vitamin pill. Jaffa cakes are good. They don't also have to be good for you.

Despite the name, there remains some debate over whether Jaffa cakes are really a cake or a biscuit. This was an important question for manufacturers, as there's a VAT charge on chocolate-covered biscuits (a luxury item) that doesn't apply to cake (a basic necessity of life). When challenged in court, the makers contended that cakes go hard when stale, while biscuits go soft, and since Jaffa cakes go hard, that makes them cakes. Thus a legal definition was born, and a potential Jaffa cake tax crisis was averted.

Some people remain unconvinced, but let's be blunt here – they are made of cake – they are cakes.

Crisps

It saddens me greatly to admit this, but despite the obvious cultural significance of crisps, they are not a British invention. No, they were invented by a Native American chef in New York State, who sliced his French fries extra thin to satisfy a customer who was complaining that his fries were too chunky. Crisps were thus invented in a country that doesn't even have the decency to call them crisps!

Neither did the British come up with the brilliant idea of adding seasonings. The initial idea to put a little blue twist of salt in the packet was first conceived in Australia, and an Irishman came up with the technology to pre-season the crisps, giving the world that enduring favourite, cheese and onion flavour.

However, it was the British who elevated the flavoured crisp to an art form and created the diversity of salty snacks we celebrate today. While the rest of the world was still limited to the most basic flavours, Britain's bold crisp pioneers were pushing forward with flavours such as prawn cocktail, Worcestershire sauce and roast beef and mustard. Foreign visitors to these islands, used to the peculiar binary choice of plain salt or paprika flavours, would be overwhelmed by the choices available here, and would often pack their suitcases with crisps to take to the folks back home.

America has since followed suit with its own peculiar flavours. However, the launch of the mango chilli crisp was the point at which things officially became just too silly.

Asparagus

Here's the great dichotomy of asparagus. On one hand it is considered a natural aphrodisiac because of its stimulating mix of vitamins and minerals, its slightly suggestive shape, and the fact that it is best eaten with fingertips and a sly wink. On the other hand, it is a diuretic that turns your pee green and makes it smell funny. Who can still find it in them to be seductive when they know they have green, smelly pee?

Leaving aside matters of the bedroom and bathroom, and sticking strictly to the kitchen, asparagus is one of the world's most decadently enjoyable vegetables. As it should always be eaten at the peak of freshness, asparagus should be bought as locally as possible. The good news is that British asparagus is probably the best in the world.

Asparagus is often regarded as a bit of a luxury item, but it is so good for you, and so simple to cook, that it should really be a regular fixture at dinnertimes during those lamentably brief eight weeks in May and June when it is in season. Asparagus is full of folic acid, fibre and potassium, and low in calories and sodium. All you need to do to cook it is steam it in an upright bundle for about three minutes, until tender, and then serve it with a blob of salted butter, which perfectly brings out its sweet, creamy flavour.

An interesting fact for word nerds: 'asparagus' is actually the Latin name for this vegetable. The English name is 'sperage', though it was sometimes known as 'sparrowgrass'.

Shortbread

The simplest of all teatime treats, shortbread is literally as easy as one, two, three. Specifically, it is one part sugar, two parts butter and three parts flour. The butter and sugar should be beaten together into a paste, and the flour is then slowly added to create pale, friable dough. The biscuits can then be rolled out into circles or squares and baked in a moderate oven until golden.

It is such an elementary recipe that shortbread is probably the first thing most children learn to cook, either at home or at school. In this case that simplicity is definitely a virtue, as the resulting biscuit is the perfect blend of gorgeous buttery richness and pleasing sugary sweetness.

Shortbread absolutely must be made with butter, of course. In fact, the rise of shortbread coincides with the rise in the popularity of butter, which was long regarded as fit only for peasants. Thankfully, we know better now. If you try to make shortbread with any other kind of fat, you'll end up with shortcake, which is infinitely inferior. Quite why you would want to make it with anything other than butter, I cannot imagine. When it comes to baking, butter is always better.

Ploughman's Lunch

Ploughman's lunch is a fraud. It is served in pubs up and down the land as traditional British fare, the name evoking images of an English pastoral idyll, where men toil in the fields all morning, then pause at midday when the women come bustling out with a fine feast of wholemeal bread, local cheese and home-made pickle. Yet research suggests that the term dates back only as far as 1960, when it was coined by the English Country Cheese Council as a way of marketing their produce.

But really, who cares? If you are looking for a simple, filling meal that brings together some of the very best that Britain has to offer, you cannot ask for much better than a tasty platter of bread, cheese and pickle. Each of these items gets its own entry in this list, but there is a particular pleasure in enjoying them all together.

A few other native specialities can be thrown into a decent ploughman's, including apples, eggs, celery, beetroot or radishes, and one might as well serve it with a big frothy pint of English ale. There really ought to be a few pickled onions in there as well, because a ploughman's lunch is really at its best with their biting tang. It is increasingly common to find the cheese in a ploughman's substituted with some thick slices of ham or a chunk of pork pie, but that sort of misses the point, and would doubtless infuriate the august members of the English Country Cheese Council.

Ploughman's lunch may well be a fraud, but it is a welcome fraud. Anyway, when you get right down to it, what do we think ploughmen actually ate for lunch back in the day? Bread, cheese and pickle would all have been available to them. I don't think they would have been popping indoors for a Pot Noodle.

FOR THE RECIPE SEE PAGE 224

Rhubarb

Rhubarb came to us from China, where it was regarded as a potent drug (a purgative for treating fever). It was in this capacity that it came to Europe in the seventeenth century, taking root not in the kitchen, but in the pharmacy. Today rhubarb is still often used as a digestive aid.

Rhubarb was also a popular ornamental plant, and it was not until quite recently in the plant's history that it came to be regarded as fit for consumption. It was of course the British who first decided to try eating it, after realising that all it took to overcome rhubarb's natural sharpness was a little sugar.

Wakefield has long been the natural home to British rhubarb, providing the right kind of soil and the right amount of rainfall for the plant to thrive. Rhubarb was big business in Yorkshire around the time of the Industrial Revolution – and a year-round business at that, thanks to the practice of 'forcing' rhubarb. This involved growing it in a dark, coal-heated shed, with the warmth encouraging growth and the darkness forcing the rhubarb to stretch in search of sunlight, creating a more delicate, succulent stem with a vibrant pink colour.

The wonderfully tart, tangy flavour of rhubarb always needs a little sweetening to bring out its best, but when properly cooked, it makes an ideal ingredient for desserts, or a perfect accompaniment to pork or duck. It is also great as a pickle, or simply sugared and roasted to make hot little jammy treats. If you don't fancy cooking it, you can always pop to the corner shop for a bag of rhubarb and custard boiled sweets.

Balti

Now we come to one of Britain's most momentous contributions to world cuisine: the curry.

The British Empire in general has been good for food, even if it has been bad for self-determination and international peace. The British high street has perhaps the most diverse collection of international restaurants anywhere in the world because we travelled all over the globe and brought all the food back home in the care of immigrant restaurateurs. In fact, if it had not been for the empire, we might all still be eating parsnips and offal for dinner every day, and that would lose its charm by about Tuesday.

The word 'curry' probably comes from the Tamil word *kari*, meaning 'sauce'. Then again, it might come from the English word 'cury', meaning 'to cook'. Either way, the dishes we recognise today as curry are a distinctly Anglo-Indian take on the native cuisines of the subcontinent, given that no one in Asia would recognise these dishes as authentic today.

The balti – a hot, quick and unfussy approach to curry – is an especially British invention, unknown in India and directly traceable to Birmingham, though there's some dispute over which curry house came up with it first. The great joy of balti, and what makes it seem so particularly British, is that it is served with bread rather than rice. Scooping up hot spicy chunks of curried meat with strips of torn naan, parathna or chapatti is a particularly shameless pleasure. It may well be the apex of civilisation.

FOR THE RECIPE SEE PAGE 224

Welsh Lamb

When I was quite small my family went on a week's holiday to a little cottage in the countryside. There was a small farm next to the cottage, where a single little new-born lamb was often seen playing in a field. We adopted this lamb as our unofficial family pet for the duration of the holiday, and we christened him Miney Mo (as in 'eenie meenie miney mo').

Soon after we got back, we had lamb for lunch one Sunday, and my sister cruelly told me that the meat we were eating was Miney Mo. It wasn't, of course, but I did not know that at the time, and the shock of it put me off eating lamb for years afterwards.

This was a terrible error in judgement on my part – think of all the many years of lovely tasty lamb that I've missed out on! Still, it brings home the fact that eating lamb is really the ultimate test of the carnivore. Once you can convince yourself to eat an irresistibly cute baby animal, there is really not much that can stop you.

The bad news for the animal kingdom is that irresistibly cute baby animals are delicious. Lamb is an especially juicy, tender meat with a fine, delicate flavour, and the best lamb is reared on the wet, verdant Welsh hills. Welsh lamb chops are excellent, roast leg of lamb is sublime, and – just between you and me – lamb also makes wonderful kebabs, though it is better to barbecue your own than to risk whatever it is they're hiding under the chilli sauce in those vans.

I don't know what became of Miney Mo, but I'm sure he was especially succulent, and I can only hope he had the dignity of being well roasted and served with mint sauce – which, as it happens, is next on this list.

FOR THE RECIPE SEE PAGE 223

Mint Sauce

Putting the sauce before the meat may seem like putting the cart before the horse, but as wonderful as lamb is, I cannot help thinking that one of the greatest pleasures of a lamb roast is having an excuse to heap a big helping of mint sauce on your plate.

Mint came to Britain with the Romans, and while we did not find as many uses for it as we did for ginger, we certainly took it to our hearts. There's not much to mint sauce: the vinegar adds tang, the sugar adds sweetness and the three flavours combine to make a sauce that is uniquely stimulating to the taste buds. It seems extraordinary that the rest of the world has never developed a taste for the stuff, as it is surely a hard sauce to beat. Its kissing cousin, mint jelly – made with pectin-rich apples to make the jelly set – is an acceptable alternative, especially when it contains big crunchy sugar crystals.

Mint sauce is presumably the reason why God put sheep on this Earth, though the wool must be considered a useful perk. The only disgrace is that there is nothing that goes half so well with mint sauce as lamb, so unless we eat lamb every day, we might never get to enjoy enough of it.

Channel Island Milk

We seem to live in an age that fears milk. Anyone trying to lose weight runs scared from it, switching to semi-skimmed or skimmed, or dropping milk from their diet altogether because of the bogeyman of saturated fat. This makes no sense to me because milk just is not fatty. Even the regular full-fat milk you find on the supermarket shelves is only 4 per cent fat at most, and most foods would love to be able to market themselves as 96 per cent fat free!

Studies now suggest that calcium is a great aid to weight loss, so drinking milk is actually good for your diet. Yet milk is still demonised, and too many people are passing up on an excellent, nutritious, natural drink that's full of goodness and protein. It is certainly possible to have too much of a good thing, but the important point to remember is that milk is, first and foremost, a very good thing.

There is one type of milk that exceeds a fat content of 4 per cent, and that's the gold-top milk of Jersey and Guernsey cows. Channel Island gold top contains a shocking – wait for it – 5.5 per cent fat! The result is a champagne among milks, with a luxuriously creamy flavour that's simply sublime. It is ideal for cooking, and makes for an especially glorious porridge or an unbeatable bowl of breakfast cereal. Channel Island gold top is becoming an endangered food because people are so terrified of milk, so do your bit to save it for future generations and buy a bottle today.

West Country Cider

On my first visit to the USA a friend offered me a glass of cider, and, being a good guest, I gladly accepted, despite my innate suspicion of American alcohol based on years of exposure to their nasty gassy lagers. Even though I believed I had braced for the worst, I wasn't prepared for the horror that I was presented with. It was just a glass of apple juice!

Americans, it seems, think cider is a non-alcoholic beverage. If you want real cider, you have to ask for 'hard cider', meaning 'alcoholic cider'. One wonders if they also refer to hot fire as 'hard fire' or tall skyscrapers as 'hard skyscrapers'.

Cider ought always to be alcoholic, and in an ideal world it ought always to be good. However, this is far from an ideal world, and cider is often terrible. The sort of cheap cider that gets sold in most supermarkets and off-licences in big brown or blue plastic bottles is of an evil and intolerable variety that verges on children's pop. It is fit only for belching competitions.

Good scrumpy cider from the West Country is a different creature altogether – a cloudy, non-carbonated, full-bodied and potent drink with an earthy, apple-rich flavour. Real cider tastes like it was made in a vat full of pig carcasses and old tractor parts – and, I'm reliably informed, it probably was. Now that's a hard cider.

Toad-in-the-Hole

Like bubble and squeak, this is one of those dishes with a name that makes tourists say things like, 'Oh, how quaint'. I am not sure what they expect it to be – perhaps they think it is the British answer to frogs' legs – but toad-in-the-hole is anything except quaint. For those unfamiliar with the concept, toad-in-the-hole consists of big fat juicy sausages in a thick, gloopy Yorkshire pudding batter, baked until toasty and brown and slathered in dark beefy gravy. It is a humble, honest meal with no hope of ever being successfully tarted up or rendered dainty by any fashionable food movement.

Apparently the toads in the original recipe were pieces of leftover meat rather than sausages. The rest of the recipe consists of everyday larder staples, making this a standby supper that can be whipped together on short notice. It is not clear when sausages took the place of leftovers in the dish, but they make perfect companions to the thick, eggy batter.

It is also not clear why the meat in the dish was named 'toads', leading generations of children to regard the dish with suspicion on their first encounter. It seems likely that no toads have ever been hurt in the making of this dish. However, some hearts may be hurt in the eating of it.

FOR THE RECIPE SEE PAGE 222

Chutney

Chutney is another product of the British Empire in India. The original chutney – or 'chatni' – was an Indian relish made from fruits and spices, and served fresh, but it came back to Britain as a cooked and preserved mango chutney called Major Grey's.

It was this preserved version, with the fruit and spices simmered in vinegar and sugar, that became the common standard – a sort of chunky savoury jam that was perfect with hot meat, cold cuts or a big chunk of pie.

Major Grey's chutney reigned supreme in Britain for years, and it is still available today, but the Victorians also came up with some thoroughly British variations on the theme, creating chutneys made from apples, apricots, rhubarb and plums (plum chutney being my personal favourite).

This British cooked version of Indian chutney has become popular all over the world, and you can now find chutneys incorporating everything from papayas to cranberries. Whatever meat you're eating, there's surely a chutney out there that will go perfectly with it, though in my experience the best chutneys are never the mass-produced ones, but the home-made ones that you have to buy at markets or beg off friends.

Hot Toddy

Winter is a time for snowball fights, log fires and frosted window panes – yet global warming seems to be robbing us of all the Dickensian charms of the season, with each winter seeming milder than the last. Before you know it, we'll be having barbecues on Christmas Day, like our endearingly degenerate antipodean cousins.

Without long, cold winter nights, we might also be in danger of losing the hot toddy, which is a particularly fine way to spice up the season. Alcohol is the lifeblood of the nation, so it stands to reason that when the world turns icy we would heat it up. It is also regarded as a particularly enjoyable way to clear the tubes when afflicted with the common cold.

A hot toddy is usually made from a healthy dram of whisky topped with boiling water, sweetened with honey or brown sugar and spiced with cloves, cinnamon and perhaps a dash of orange or lemon juice. Some prefer to use rum or brandy, and during Christmas week a port toddy can be just the ticket.

Whichever variety of booze is used, the drink should be enjoyed at leisure, in the warm, perhaps under a blanket. The intoxicating vapours should be allowed to rise up and envelop you so that they can fill your head with cosy dreams, and the drink itself should slip into your bones and warm you from the inside out. If mild winters mean an end to hot toddies, bring back the freezing cold.

Chip Butty

The chip butty is perhaps the trashiest food ever produced in these fair isles, and quite deliberately so. It is consciously, conspicuously and gloriously lowbrow food, a shamelessly undignified way to combine two forms of starchy carbohydrate into one miraculous life-affirming indulgence. Chip buttyness is next to godliness.

The recipe for a good chip butty is quite simple. Take one portion of chips, squeeze as many of them as you can into a white bread roll or between two slices of buttered white bread, add sauce, salt and vinegar to taste, and enjoy. The bread should, of course, be of the cheap and cheerful variety – there is no place for healthy wholemeal when it comes to a good old-fashioned chip sandwich. The butter is also important because you want the hot chips to melt the butter into the bread.

While it is entirely possible to make a decent chip butty at home, it is far better to go to the local chip shop and order one there – or just order the chips and do the complicated sandwich-making part yourself so that you can be sure it is made to your exact specifications. The resulting sandwich should have a strange alchemical effect on the brain, sending out a signal that says, 'I'm happy now. Let's always feel this way.' And you could if you wanted 'always' to be a very short time indeed.

I should mention that there is one alternative to the chip butty that's perhaps even more sordid, and that's the crisp sandwich, but it is not the sort of thing that should be talked about in polite society.

Treacle Tart

When I was a child, treacle tart was my favourite food in the whole world. It is an incredible sugar hit with a hint of zesty citrus, and it is a rarity among British puddings in that it is arguably as good with ice cream as it is with custard. There is definitely something special about watching a big dollop of thick vanilla ice cream melt into the steaming hot treacle goo.

The first time I made treacle tart I was a little alarmed to discover what it is actually made of. First of all, it is not actually treacle, though that is really rather obvious when you look at it – it is not dark enough to be British treacle, which is a little like tarmac made of sugar. Instead, it is made with golden syrup, which is much lighter in colour and somewhat sweeter in flavour. It might once have been made with black treacle, and probably still could be, but golden syrup seems to have won over in most people's preferences.

Second, and in common with so much else on this list, it is made from bread. The filling is a mixture of golden syrup and breadcrumbs. Everyone else in the world may already have been aware of this fact, but it somehow passed me by and took me completely by surprise. This means that treacle tart is actually a rather frugal sort of dish – I had always regarded it as the utmost in old-fashioned luxury, and I probably always will. Treacle tart is not my favourite food any more, but I still don't think I could ever in good conscience say no to a slice.

FOR THE RECIPE SEE PAGE 221

Saffron Cake

When it comes to festive food, Christmas seems to get more than its fair share. Easter has to make do with just a few specialities. Chocolate eggs are always welcome, of course, and the smell of hot cross buns seems to me to be intensely evocative of springtime. Then there are the cakes. Simnel cake, with its eleven marzipan balls to represent the eleven loyal apostles, seems just a bit too zealous for afternoon tea. I much prefer a lovely Cornish saffron loaf.

Saffron is one of the world's most exotic and evocative spices. Hand-plucked from the heart of a crocus that only flowers for three weeks of the year, it is extremely fragile and very expensive to produce – but just a couple of strands are packed with enough of saffron's vibrant, earthy musk to create a buttery, golden yellow cake. Airy, raisin-rich saffron cake is basically your classic fruit cake with a Rolls-Royce engine. Just beware of imitations: saffron is so pricey that it is not unusual for people to try to fake it with safflower or vanilla, and the result is not the same at all.

In the Middle Ages saffron was so highly prized that people were burnt at the stake for trying to fake it. Britain tried to create its own saffron industry, which is where the tradition of Cornish saffron cake arose from, but we never had the right climate for it and the industry eventually died out. However, while saffron is not really British, we were probably the first to think it was a good idea to bake a cake with it.

Pie and Mash

Pie and mash sounds like a bit of a vague concept. The mash part of the equation is fairly easy to grasp, and I don't see any reason to be a potato purist. One might well prefer some parsnip or cheese in one's mash, or a bit of colcannon, and I'm personally very partial to mashed swede. Then there's the question of how thoroughly you mash your potato. Some like it puréed or pressed through a ricer, while I like my potatoes roughly smashed and slightly lumpy, with lots of cream and butter.

Pie, though, is an altogether more ambiguous proposition. It has to be a savoury pie, of course, and it has to be a pastry pie (there is no point having a potato-topped pie alongside more mashed potato), but beyond that just about anything goes. Steak and kidney is probably the great British favourite, though I'd happily swap the kidney in my pie for some ale. Others might prefer a pie with chicken, lamb, fish, eel, mushroom or even corned beef. Whatever your preference, there's a pie and mash for everyone.

Yet the most iconic pie and mash is the East End version – a pale and soggy little pie containing a sinister minced mystery meat, served with an ice-cream scoop or two of powdery mashed potato, a ladleful of that strange, thin parsley sauce called 'liquor', and a bottle of dark brown vinegar incongruously stuffed with chillies. It doesn't sound terribly appetising, and it doesn't look all that appealing, but there's a weird and wonderful magic going on in those dingy little East End pie shops, and it is certainly an experience worth having.

FOR THE RECIPE SEE PAGE 221

Boiled Egg and Soldiers

This is your basic boiled egg with a side order of military intervention.

When compiling this list, I faced an agonising choice over which method for cooking eggs was the most quintessentially British. Fried eggs are obviously a favourite, especially when served at a greasy spoon, but they're hardly a unique idea. Scrambled eggs have a certain classy appeal, but they really belong to the French, and poached eggs, as featured in eggs Benedict, seem terribly American.

No, the most British way to eat an egg is soft-boiled, in an egg cup, with a plate of buttered soldiers. Quite how these dunkable strips of bread picked up their military epithet is not quite clear, but the best guess anyone seems able to make is that it is because they sit in a regimented rank on the plate.

The only war these soldiers will ever face is over the question of whether or not to toast the bread. Those who believe in toasting their soldiers argue that it gives the bread more rigidity, making it easier to scoop out the delicious runny yolk. Those who prefer their soldiers untoasted point out that they can better absorb the yolk into the bread. Both sides of the argument are firmly entrenched in their views, and never the twain shall meet.

Whichever way you prefer your soldiers, it is my humble opinion that the world would be a much happier place if all our soldiers were made of bread. But not our air force pilots because then the planes would crash.

Scotch Broth

Britain is not a great soup-making nation. That, once again, is a French area of special expertise. However, most of the good soups that we can claim were created up in Scotland, including cock-a-leekie, cullen skink and this enduring classic – and any single one of them could take a French soup in a fight.

Usually the word 'broth' is used to denote a thin sort of soup, strained of all the ingredients that gave it its flavour to leave a shimmering golden liquor. This broth can then be used as the basis for soup or sauce, or eaten just as it is.

Despite its name, Scotch broth does not belong to this dainty class. After all, this is a soup that hails from the cold and blustery Scottish Highlands, where nothing that might be eaten would ever get thrown away. The slow-cooked chunks of mutton, the fat pearls of barley and the generous helpings of tasty veg that give Scotch broth its flavour are all kept in the pot, making for a hefty, filling and wonderfully warming meal in a bowl. The only way anything ever gets to leave a Scotch broth is in a spoon.

FOR THE RECIPE SEE PAGE 220

Fruit Fool

Fruit fool is a blissfully unpretentious idea, combining the best of Britain's native fruits with the finest cream from our dairies into one of the most decadent desserts imaginable. It is made by heating the fruit with sugar and half-heartedly folding the resulting syrup into soft whipped cream. The lack of serious effort when it comes to stirring the fruit and cream together is a vitally important part of the process – fruit fool should always be marbled and uneven in appearance. It should never look like any real hard work went into it. It is a haphazard hodgepodge of a pudding, a gorgeous ripple of pure indulgence made all the better by a frivolous lack of care.

Classic fools are made with the sort of tart fruits that grow so well in our hedgerows and gardens, most notably gooseberries and rhubarb: the contrast between the sharp and creamy flavours creates a sensation of absolute pleasure. That said, there is probably not a fruit in the world that does not benefit from a generous swirl of cream.

The name, incidentally, is taken from the French *fouler*, meaning 'to mash'. There's nothing the least bit stupid about a fruit fool, though it is reassuringly simple.

FOR THE RECIPE SEE PAGE 220

Aberdeen Angus

It is a well-known fact that a vegetarian is simply someone who prefers to eat their meat in private. Everyone loves meat, after all – it would simply be too strange not to eat it. Everyone especially loves cow meat because cows make for such very meaty meat, so big and juicy and full of flavour.

Aberdeen Angus is recognised world-wide as one of the tastiest breeds of cow – to the extent that certain fast food chains are even trying to turn their reputations around by introducing Angus burgers.

The Aberdeen Angus is the work-cow of excellent meats because it is such an affable, adaptable beast; it grows up fast and has plenty of meat to offer, so it does not take long for a new calf to grow up into lots of lovely fat steaks. In fact, the Angus is such an agreeable cow that it would probably slaughter itself if only it knew how much the effort would be appreciated. It is a cow that wants to be eaten. Probably.

The Angus originated in Scotland, but it is now a world-wide breed. Even so, beef of British origin is still among the best – and the safest – that money can buy. Angus is increasingly commonplace, but we must not let familiarity breed contempt. Instead, we should just breed more cows. Lovely, delicious cows.

FOR THE RECIPE SEE PAGE 220

Bread Pudding

Bread and butter pudding was up there at number 80, but this other great bread-based pud comes in 33 places higher because as good as bread and butter pudding is, this one is just that much better.

Bread pudding is thicker, fatter, darker and heavier, with a crisp brown crust glistening with sugar and spotted with little raisins that blacken like coal in the oven. It is, in a word, stodgy. By comparison, bread and butter pudding seems almost light and Continental, with all its funny ideas about croissants and fresh fruit. Bread and butter pudding can be turned into something gourmet. Bread pudding has no such aspirations, and stubbornly resists change. It is a frugal way to turn leftovers into afters, and it remains solidly grounded in its roots of stale bread and suet. Food does not get much more down-to-earth and humble than this.

A word of caution: if you are going to eat bread pudding, you should make sure you do not have anything important to do afterwards because this pudding is going to sit in your stomach like a lead weight. But it is a price worth paying for such a life-affirming treat. Bread pudding is also traditional fare in the southern USA, where they call it 'soul food'. That is as good a name for it as any.

FOR THE RECIPE SEE PAGE 219

Wholegrain Bread

Some people like brown bread, some prefer white. It doesn't really matter either way, since they're usually exactly the same bread, one coloured and the other bleached. However, traditional wholegrain bread is another matter — that's bread for people who care about what they are eating.

Supermarket shelves these days are heaving with dozens of different chemically molested, ready-sliced, flavourless and nutritionally deficient prepackaged breads, which seems to suggest that someone out there is buying this awful junk, and they cannot all be using it for chip butties and fried slices.

Wholegrain bread is rich with vitamins, minerals and fibre, and it is also a great source of slow-burning energy. On top of that, while most modern breads do not taste of anything much at all, wholegrain has a delicious nutty, wheaty flavour that makes it perfect for toast and the ideal complement to marmalade, eggs or beans. It is also great with a bowl of soup — wholesome and filling and unlikely to fall apart when dipped — and it tastes fantastic just as it comes with a generous smear of butter.

That is not to say that wholegrain is the ideal bread for everything. Since it is so full of flavour, it should be avoided in recipes that require bread just for bulk, including most bread-based puddings. The rest of the time, however, I'm not sure why you would bother with anything else. The people of Britain need to be reminded that bread is not just a way to keep your fingers dry when you're eating a sandwich. Bread is food, and it can be truly excellent food, so eat well.

Porter

Thanks to Guinness, stout has become a much more famous dark beer than porter – yet stout is to porter as *Knots Landing* is to *Dallas*. Porter is the original liquid bread, and stout is just a latter-day spin-off.

The origins of porter are as murky as the beer itself, but the romantic version is that it was first created in a London pub frequented by street porters, who would stop off for a pint as they carried their packages to and fro. The beer was popular with these working men because it was so substantial and fortifying.

Whatever the truth of it, porter was the first British beer to become popular up and down the country – not because it travelled particularly well, but because its dark colour and strong roasted flavour could hide a multitude of sins. Once upon a time, porter was huge business. In fact, in 1814 a giant vat of porter in a brewery on Tottenham Court Road split open and flooded the streets with hundreds of thousands of gallons of porter, destroying two houses and killing eight people. And still people raced into the streets with buckets to drink free beer from the gutter.

Porter eventually gave birth to the still-darker and stronger stout, and while stout thrived in Ireland, English porter was hit by a grain shortage during the First World War and slowly died out. Most people today have never heard of porter, but I grew up near a pub that brewed its own, so I've always been very fond of the stuff. It seems to have enjoyed a slow resurgence in recent years, but it is probably not going to flood the streets again any time soon.

Shepherd's Pie

There is some debate in the world over which is better – shepherd's pie or cottage pie? A third party exists that does not seem to know there is a difference. And then there is a fourth party that doesn't really care, just so long as there is pie. Their party is the most fun.

For those not in the know, shepherd's pie is minced lamb with a mashed potato topping. Cottage pie is the same thing, but with beef instead of lamb. Cottage pie is obviously a perfectly delightful dish, and it has the longer pedigree, but there are more than enough minced beef dishes in the world already. Minced lamb, with rosemary and onions and a 'crust' of browned potato, is really something special. Even better, if you want a powerfully meaty pie, you can make shepherd's pie with mutton – an underrated meat that is currently enjoying an overdue revival; slow-cooked for a strong, rich flavour, mutton makes for an exceptionally filling dinner. However, mutton is still uncommon enough that you may have to ask your butcher to order it specially.

I have heard it said that shepherd's pie was once made with lambs' tails sticking out of the topping, which is so beautifully macabre that I can only hope that it is true. The other thing I always liked about shepherd's pie as a child was the idea that it might contain actual shepherds. If you buy your pie from some of the nastier budget supermarkets, this is still a distinct possibility.

FOR THE RECIPE SEE PAGE 219

Fish and Chips

I was raised in Hastings, one of the great British seaside towns, and home to a struggling fishing industry. Despite this childhood proximity to the sea, it took me a long time to develop a taste for fish, perhaps because I was always slightly scared of the gnarled, wind-whipped, gap-toothed sea-gypsies that dragged in the daily catch on Hastings' stony beaches. Sometimes it is best not to see how the food gets to your plate, or who helped get it there.

I am over such prissiness now, of course, and on hot summer days back home I am more than happy to head down to the seafront and order a big, fat battered fish on a bed of vinegary chips, all wrapped up in greasy paper. It is best eaten on the promenade, where you can sit on a bench and happily stuff yourself into a salty, starchy coma of happiness.

These days, thanks to hygiene restrictions, you cannot get your fish and chips wrapped in old newspaper. Obviously, this means that it will never quite taste the same as it ought to because the effects of a hot steamed newspaper always adds a certain indefinable *je ne c'est quoi*. It also means that you are robbed of the chance to read the cartoons or the football scores (or the FTSE index, if you were very unlucky) while you enjoy your supper.

FOR THE RECIPE SEE PAGE 218

Green Ginger Wine

We all remember where we were when the clock ticked over from 1999 to 2000, unless we were far too drunk. I was on Blackfriar's Bridge overlooking the Thames in the drizzling rain, pressed into a crush of bodies and swigging green ginger wine from the bottle. The fireworks were pretty good. The ginger wine was better.

Ginger wine is a remarkable winter warmer. It is a heartening, spicy and distinctly Christmassy elixir made from raisins and ginger, with a consistency somewhere between sherry and syrup. It may have medicinal qualities, or it may just be that the hit of ginger is enough to make you believe that it has medicinal qualities, but sometimes that's good enough. I certainly would not want to try to get through the winter blues without it. For an extra kick it can be mixed with scotch to create a whisky mac, a very fine drink that has sadly fallen out of fashion. I have tried to explain the concept to every barman in London, but as soon as they seem to have grasped it, they end up moving back to Australia.

As Britain has never had much success at making real wine, we have made repeated attempts over the years to come up with a viable alternative using just about every plant under the sun, including cowslip, elderflower and dandelion. Most of these strange concoctions are thankfully relegated to basement brews, but ginger wine has survived on the market for over 250 years. You cannot argue with success.

Peas

Poor old peas are perhaps the most under-appreciated of beans. They have a reputation for being boring and mundane, and seem to be forever associated with suburban drudgery and conservative palates. Yet I've put peas higher on my list than any other vegetable because I happen to think that they are utterly wonderful, and it is long past time that they got the appreciation they deserve.

You could be forgiven for hating peas if all you have ever known of them are those dreary grey shrivelled lumps that take up space on your plate, waiting to be thrown away at the end of the meal. I do not know what those things are, but they are certainly not peas. They are probably the work of food terrorists.

Real peas are sweet, vibrant, bright green miracles of flavour and goodness. They ought always to be plump, glossy and beautiful, sitting proudly on your plate like a delicious, vitamin-rich miniature re-creation of our green and pleasant land.

The problem with peas is that people overcook them. While most frozen vegetables will unavoidably turn into flavourless mush when you cook them, frozen peas can actually look and taste great, provided you ignore the packet instructions and cook them for about a minute in roiling, boiling water. Fresh peas do not need to be cooked at all, of course, and they are wonderful to eat raw by the handful. Peas also make one of the finest, thickest, most satisfying soups known to man.

Peas are clearly in need of a cultural reappraisal. They deserve your respect and admiration. I suppose all I'm saying is, give peas a chance... I am so sorry.

Flapjack

The flapjack is another area of potential transatlantic confusion, as those funny Americans are under the impression that a flapjack is a type of pancake. Yet every British schoolchild knows that a flapjack is a delicious tray-baked cake made from golden syrup, oats and butter.

I will let you in on a shameful secret. The Americans are actually right – they can claim the precedent here. In Britain the word 'flapjack' referred to a type of pancake as far back as the fourteenth century, long before it was ever used to describe our popular oaty confection, and long before any rogue Britons accidentally kick-started America. We like to think that Americans are sullying our language, but a lot of the time they're preserving old English words that we've abandoned. It was the English who invented 'fall' to describe autumn, for example, and the Americans took the U out of words like colour and honour because we only added them to try to look more fancy.

Still, the British have a perfectly good word for pancakes, and there aren't any other words for flapjack – and if we don't have a word for something, maybe we won't get to eat it any more, so it is best that we keep the name where it now belongs.

In America the closest thing they have to a flapjack is a granola bar, and that's some sort of terrible health food. Flapjacks are too good to be healthy. They're comfort food with an indulgent, enveloping flavour that you could very nearly curl up and fall asleep in.

FOR THE RECIPE SEE PAGE 218

Porridge

I was a sucker for sugary cereals in the days of my callow youth. For me it was all about Sugar Puffs, Ricicles and Crunchy Nut Cornflakes, and I was so addicted to Frosties that I sent off for membership of the Tony the Tiger fan club so that I could get a holographic ID card and a little toy coupé with tiger stripes. The one cereal you couldn't get me to eat was porridge. It wasn't glazed, it did not have a big-eyed spokes-character, and there was no fan club.

Tastes change, and now I am a sensible grown-up and porridge is my breakfast cereal of choice. What makes porridge so great is its extraordinary versatility. It can be made with water, milk, soy, cream or even yoghurt, and it can be flavoured with sugar, salt, syrup, cinnamon, nutmeg, jam or fruit, and that's really just the start. The only limit is your imagination – and perhaps good taste. I understand real Scotsmen never add anything to their porridge, but I've never been good at dour self-denial.

Porridge can be the healthiest, most energising start to the day, or it can be a wicked indulgence to put you in the best possible mood for dealing with Monday morning. In truth, it shouldn't be possible to dislike porridge. At worst it might be too hot or too cold, but otherwise, it is just right.

FOR THE RECIPE SEE PAGE 218

Maldon Salt

Of all the places that one might expect to find a world-class culinary ingredient, an estuary in Essex is probably not high on the list; yet that is exactly where the world's best salt comes from.

For hundreds of years the people of Maldon have filtered sea salt from the spring tides of the Blackwater estuary, boiling off the water to leave behind the delicate flakes of crystal salt, which are then harvested by hand. Maldon sea salt has established itself as the gold standard for serious chefs thanks to its satisfyingly crisp crystals and delicate, sea-fresh taste. It is an impressively robust flavour enhancer, and Delia and Nigella both swear by it.

Health experts are rightly concerned about the amount of salt that we are consuming these days, as manufacturers are adding excessive quantities to the food they produce, and consumers are typically adding still more at the table. If you are serious about reducing your salt intake, Maldon salt may be the way to go, as a little pinch goes a lot further than ordinary salt. On the other hand, Maldon salt tastes so good on everything that you may even end up putting it on your ice cream. (It has been tried, and apparently it is very good.)

If you want to be a really serious salt snob, you don't just need the salt, you also need the salt pig – a convenient wide-mouthed ceramic pot that allows you to reach in and grab a pinch, then break it down with your fingertips. Then you can lick your fingers and discover how good you taste as well.

Chicken Tikka Masala

The late Robin Cook hailed chicken tikka masala as a British national dish and an icon of British cultural integration. As he rightly pointed out in his speech in 2001, chicken tikka hails from India, but the addition of masala sauce is what makes it British because the British love to put sauce on everything. The resulting dish is a triumph of multiculturalism that is now so popular in Britain that Marks & Spencer is reported to sell 18 tonnes of chicken tikka masala a week in its sandwiches alone.

No one knows exactly who invented chicken tikka masala, though many restaurants around the country like to claim that honour. The typical story goes that a patron at a Bangladeshi restaurant sent his chicken tikka back to the kitchen because it did not have any gravy, so the chef poured on a can of tomato soup, and a legend was born.

The word *masala* simply means 'mixed spices', so there's no set recipe for masala sauce. The basics are consistent – marinated chicken in a tomato sauce – but the spiciness and the creaminess can vary wildly, and sometimes even cream of coconut is added. The chicken tikka masala you order in one restaurant could be completely different from the one you would order in the restaurant next door.

Yet despite this variability – Robin Cook might have called it diversity – it has become perhaps the most widely popular Indian dish in the world – everywhere, that is, except in the Indian subcontinent, where it is still largely unknown.

FOR THE RECIPE SEE PAGE 217

Stinking Bishop

One of my favourite places to visit in all the world is Neal's Yard Dairy in Covent Garden, London. It is a cheese-lover's paradise, with a glorious rich, pungent smell that I could happily submerge myself in, though it seems to overpower some visitors, as foreign tourists can often be seen running from the shop with fingers pinching their noses. Neal's Yard is like Disneyland for the true gourmet, and I like to imagine that its employees are the happiest people on Earth because they get to spend every day in the company of Colston Bassett, Beenleigh Blue, Doddington, Ragstone and Stinking Bishop.

Stinking Bishop, as you might expect, has a rather ripe smell, not unlike a drunken hobo. Like Double Gloucester it is made from the milk of the Gloucester cow, but it is an altogether different type of cheese – runny and richly creamy, with a lip-smacking delicious flavour that is much milder than the stench would suggest.

The name Stinking Bishop, though an apt marker of one of the cheese's most distinctive characteristics, is actually second-hand. The original Stinking Bishop was a type of pear, and the cider made from this fruit was used to wash the rind of the cheese, imparting its extraordinary aroma in the process. Actually, to be strictly accurate, the original stinking bishop was the person who cultivated the pears, a man named Bishop with a stinking temper, who clearly was not well loved by the neighbours who renamed his pears. Both the man and his fruit have been rightly eclipsed in their fame by the cheese.

Wiltshire Ham

The islands of Hawaii were left with a surplus of Spam when the GIs headed home after the war in the Pacific, and Spam has been a part of Hawaii's national cuisine ever since.

There were American GIs in Wiltshire too, but the locals there did not seem to develop the same affection for chopped pork in a can, and for good reason. They had the finest real ham right there on their doorstep. Hawaii may get all the hot sun, the hula dancing and the tropical rum cocktails, but does it have a wealth of Wiltshire ham? No it does not.

Wiltshire ham is slowly brine-cured and matured on the bone to create beautifully pink, succulent meat with a full yet mellow flavour. Beer, mustard or brown sugar is sometimes added to the curing process to add extra depth. While most warm, sunny countries prefer to dry-cure their ham – as with Italian prosciutto, Spanish serrano or German Black Forest ham – we in mild, rainy Britain like our ham to be as wet as our weather.

There are two great things to do with wet-cured ham, other than serving it baked. You can fry it with eggs for a simple supper, or you can roll thick slices of it into a bap with a little lettuce and a lot of mustard.

Note, however, that you should not confuse Wiltshire ham with the town of Ham in Wiltshire, which is very picturesque but somewhat hard on the teeth.

Crumpets

Hot buttered crumpet. Oh, but you're a naughty little thing.

The teatime delight we know as the crumpet is a versatile, spongy little puck of baked dough, but the word 'crumpet' also has a second meaning. It's a saucy seaside postcard sort of word, used to describe a person of particularly comely appearance. It used to be applied only to women, but in these more enlightened times it's thrown around more liberally. Men and women alike can be basely objectified as a tasty bit of crumpet.

I'm not sure how the word came to earn its slang meaning. It was probably first used as a term of affection – like calling someone 'sweetie' – before taking on a more salacious tone. Another theory suggests that it derives from 'strumpet', which is a far less flattering word, but no less delightful to say. Crumpet strumpet crumpet.

There is something a little sordidly sensual about crumpets. If you try eating them cold and plain, they're a tedious and unrewarding experience, but as soon as you toast them and smother them with butter, they become sublimely indulgent and at least a little bit improper. The hot, salty butter melts into the crumpet, oozing out of the little holes as you bite through the warm dough, and as often as not the butter will dribble obscenely down your chin. It's probably the most risqué activity you can get away with during high tea at the Savoy.

In a sense, crumpets are just a hot butter delivery mechanism; whatever else I put on my crumpet (and it usually comes down to a choice between jam and Marmite), I always start with butter. A word of warning, though: there's an art to toasting the perfect crumpet. It needs to be hot all the way through, but don't let it get hard and crunchy on the outside. Good crumpet should be soft like a cushion, hot like a kiss and wantonly enticing – like a tasty bit of crumpet.

Sticky Toffee Pudding

There was a woman called Mrs Bumstead at my first school. She wore an aquamarine gingham pinny, she called everyone 'my lover', and she was universally popular for one very good and very simple reason: she was the head dinner lady, and she got to serve us our sponge pudding at lunchtime. Not that the puddings were anything particularly special, mind you, but they sufficed for the purposes of five-year-olds.

Let's face it, school puddings do not have to be gourmet delights to earn a place in anyone's nostalgic affections; they just need to be smothered in custard. The British remain devoted to the puddings of yore, and you can easily please a Briton by laying a plate of steaming hot sponge pudding in front of him.

As I have mentioned before, there is no spotted dick or jam roly-poly on my list, but I have left room for the best of breed. I find, as a general rule in life, it is always wise to leave room for the dark, moist, rich and oozing delicacy that is sticky toffee pudding, regardless of whether or not there's any sticky toffee pudding in the vicinity. After all, you can never be sure.

Sticky toffee pudding is so decadent, indecent and hedonistic that it probably should not even be served to children. It tastes so heavenly that it is like having a handwritten note from God saying that you have been excused from being good today.

FOR THE RECIPE SEE PAGE 216

Tablet

When Moses came down from Mount Sinai he was carrying two tablets that bore the commandments of God. Unfortunately for him, neither of the tablets was made from a delicious crumbly mix of sugar, butter and cream. Frankly, between you and me, I think God did him a bit of a disservice.

Tablet is fudge's less well-known Scottish cousin. In fact, there's very little difference between fudge – invented in the USA in the late nineteenth century – and tablet – invented in Scotland in the early eighteenth century – except that tablet has a grainier texture. It melts in the mouth just the same way, and it is also just as dangerous to make – boiling sugar can be like an angry volcano god. If you can appease the god without having to make a human sacrifice, you'll have your divine reward in the form of a tray full of tooth-rotting, creamy pale brown sweets.

Another thing that tablet shares in common with fudge is that modern recipes tend to forgo the cream in favour of sweetened condensed milk – that sickly sweet beige gloop in a can – because it can withstand much higher temperatures. On the Continent they don't bother to make tablet or fudge – they just squeeze condensed milk out of little pyramid packets directly into their mouths. And these people take pride in their cuisine! After some consideration, I think I am happier with tablet.

Rice Pudding

Milk has a magical ability to calm and soothe the anxious mind. Indeed, a glass of hot milk before bedtime is one of the most popular ways to ensure a peaceful night's sleep. It seems that the same strange alchemy must be at work in rice pudding, which is basically hot milk plumped up to the soft, effort-free consistency of baby food. For added sorcery, you can add a hypnotically aromatic sprinkle of nutmeg, cinnamon or clove.

The peculiar thing about rice pudding is that while it is undeniably very traditional and British indeed, it is also quite coincidentally very Spanish, very Indian, very Eastern European, very Latin American, very North American and very Arabian. The notion of cooking rice in milk is one that seems to have occurred to every civilisation in the world. Perhaps it is ingrained into human nature? After all, rice pudding is the ultimate comfort food. Its warm, milky loveliness is as cosy and reassuring as an old familiar blanket.

The popularity of rice pudding in Britain surely owes something to the Second World War, when its cheapness and simplicity were obvious virtues; in fact, it is fair to say that many of today's great British dishes were born out of necessity and austerity. Rice pudding continues to serve a vital purpose for the parsimonious: it is a great way to deal with leftovers when you inevitably cook too much rice to go with your curry.

Strawberries

There are many things that the British are very good at. We produce fine writers and actors and engineers and TV chefs, and blessed are our cheesemakers. What we are not at all good at is making sportsmen. Oh, we can win at darts or snooker, provided that no other countries decide to get involved, but when it comes to actual sports, we are hopeless.

We are especially bad at tennis. We can cheer on our tennis players, with only the slightest hint of resigned desperation creeping into our voices, but when it comes to actually playing tennis, we are terrible at it. Given that we host the world's premier tennis competition, it is a little embarrassing. We would probably have given up on Wimbledon years ago but for one important thing: it is indelibly linked in our minds to strawberries and cream, and strawberries are among those things that we are really very good at.

Personally, I prefer not to watch any tennis at all during Wimbledon fortnight, though I am never entirely able to avoid it. Yet just as I know I will always eat a mince pie at Christmas, I also know that I will always eat strawberries and cream during Wimbledon. Strawberries are at their best for only a very short time, so the tennis serves as a useful prompt to remind one to go out and get some while they are supremely succulent and sweet. Naturally, one should always buy British – one should always support the home team.

Pickle

Much of the history of cooking comes down to a history of food preservation. Long before we developed pasteurisation and refrigeration, the methods for keeping food fit for consumption tended to be a lot more flavourful. Salting has given us anchovies, ewe's milk cheese, peanuts and pastrami. Smoking has long been a good way to add longevity and flavour to cheeses, meats and fish. Fermentation is the basis for bread, cheese, wine and beer, and oil has popularly been used to store sauces, vegetables and spices.

Then there is pickling, which is a method of preservation that we seem to be particularly fond of in Britain. In fact, we have developed such a fondness for the taste of food steeped in seasoned vinegar – including gherkins, pickled onions and even pickled eggs – that we created a sharp, sweet, crunchy, all-purpose relish and dubbed it – with elegant simplicity – 'pickle'. Suddenly, sandwiches could be made properly for the first time in history, and after a mere thousand years or so, Cheddar cheese had found its natural partner.

Despite its generic name, there is really only one pickle, Branston, which was created over 80 years ago in the village of Branston in Staffordshire. The pickle is made with apple, marrow, dates, brown sugar and swede (inexplicably listed on the ingredients by its American name, rutabaga), but the exact formula is a closely guarded secret.

Gressingham Duck

There was a time in my life where I lived among the ducks much as Jane Goodall lived among the chimpanzees. Well, sort of. I was at the University of York, but I was not there to study ducks; I was there to study for my degree. However, the campus doubles as a wildfowl reserve, populated throughout the summer months by ducks, geese, swans and grebe. I remember the geese being a particularly unsettling presence, standing around in angry herds like surviving dinosaurs. The ducks were disturbing in another way, quacking outside my window in the early morning and ruining my lie-in.

According to campus legend, a student was once expelled from the university when a duck's legs and beak were found in his bin by a university cleaner. He had captured, killed and eaten a duck, perhaps in revenge for all the noise. Or perhaps he did it because ducks are delicious.

Gressingham duck is the most delicious of all. Its strong, gamey flavour is a cross between that of wild mallard and Peking duck and the bird is noted for its plump, succulent breast. It is a pricey piece of meat, but each and every mouthful is worth it. In a world where you can get salmon in a can and exotic desserts from a freezer, Gressingham duck still feels like a luxury.

FOR THE RECIPE SEE PAGE 216

Lemon Curd

The ingredients of a shop-bought lemon curd include modified maize starch, margarine, beta-carotene and glucose-fructose syrup. The ingredients of a home-made lemon curd are lemon juice and zest, butter, sugar and eggs. Shop-bought lemon curd is the colour of mustard and has a texture reminiscent of jelly. Home-made lemon curd is closer in colour to hollandaise and closer in texture to cream. Shop-bought lemon curd tastes synthetic and faded. Home-made lemon curd tastes fresh and zingy.

Perhaps the biggest difference, though, is that buying lemon curd in a shop is a really boring thing to do. Making your own lemon curd is a joyful experience: it is so quick and easy to whisk the ingredients together, and the thick, smooth, zesty curd thickens before your eyes. I love making lemon curd – it is one of the great simple pleasures in life. Watching other people enjoy your home-made lemon curd is another. That sharp, buttery taste is incredibly satisfying.

I usually eat lemon curd on buttered toast or scones, but it is unspeakably good in tarts and cakes, especially sandwiched in a lemon drizzle cake. You can even eat it straight from the jar. You shouldn't, of course, but you really should.

Whisky

I am sure many people will consider it a crime that whisky is not placed higher in my list – which is well and good because lists like this are no fun if you cannot find something to vehemently disagree with. Many of my friends consider a fine whisky dram to be one of the utmost pleasures in life – and possibly they are right – but there are other pleasures I appreciate more. One reason that whisky doesn't crack my top ten is that there is another spirit that I prefer. Another reason is that, by my own admission, I have not fully graduated from whisky school.

Whisky, you see, is not just a drink. It is a secret society. Those bottles you see next to the cigarettes in Tesco, those are not really whisky; neither are those upside-down bottles behind the bar in your average boozer. No, to experience real whisky you have to enter into the strange and elusive twilight world of specialist shops, where you will be required to part with an arm and a leg for a bottle of something with an unpronounceable guttural name, which you will then take home and savour, sipping it late at night from a crystal glass shaped like a tulip.

Even then, the whisky will probably be wasted on you unless you've been fully inducted into the ways of tasting. Whisky aficionados must develop a Zen mastery of their taste buds that develops only with time if they truly want to appreciate the complex flavours of peat, caramel, iodine, hay, honey, oak, bracken, butter, smoke, linseed, lemon or pepper that might be lurking in every glass. Whisky, you see, is not for ordinary mortals. It is an elite order, and I fear I am still strictly a white belt.

Brambles

Technically, a bramble is anything from the Rubus strand of the rose family, which includes raspberries, loganberries and cloudberries, but to my mind, 'bramble' means only one thing: blackberries.

When I was a kid my favourite thing about going for walks in the British countryside – apart from the smell of distant bonfires and the chance to clamber over a stile and feel rustic – was stumbling across a tangle of wild bramble bushes and searching for a few fat, juicy, glossily perfect blackberries to stain my tongue with. On really sunny days the brambles were even a little warm from the sun, and it was always worth a few scratches from the thorns.

Brambles have been growing in Britain since prehistoric times, and as a result they have had plenty of time to ingrain themselves in our folklore. The fruits were said to cure warts and coughs, while the leaves were thought to be good for diarrhoea and bleeding gums. It was also said the Devil would piss or spit on the fruits at the end of September, making them unfit to eat thereafter, which is the surest sign of the Devil's wickedness.

Although there is no better way to enjoy blackberries than in the wild, no sane man would object to enjoying them in a crumble or a pie, either on their own or with their great natural British bedfellow, Bramley apples. The blackberry is a taste that ties us to our countryside; it is the God-given manna of the British Isles.

Brown Sauce

My youngest sister and I could never see eye to eye on sauce. She was a ketchup addict, adding it to everything and anything – she even put it on her baked beans, which is surely some sort of deviant behaviour. I personally never developed much of a taste for ketchup; I've always found that it makes everything taste too sugary – but I am a lifelong fan of brown sauce.

Where this really becomes a divisive issue is in the matter of bacon sandwiches. There are actually people in the world who think bacon sandwiches should be made with ketchup, and the scary thing is that these people look just like you and me. In fact, for all I know, you could even be one of them.

I suspect the thing that scares these heretics away from the one true sauce is the ambiguity of its name. Most sauces are named after their ingredients, not for their colour. Brown sauce gives nothing away about what it might contain – it only tells you what you already know. Even today I am not entirely clear what is in it. I know it contains fruit and spices, but that's evasively vague. Vinegar is certainly a distinctive element of the flavour – and then there's the mysterious tamarind, the peculiar brown, peanut-shaped fruit of a Madagascan tree. You can see how conservative palates might opt for the safety of the familiar tomato over the exotic strangeness of the tamarind.

Yet I will not let any other sauce than brown touch the bacon in my sandwiches, and it is also my choice of sauce for eggs, chips or sausages. And it has to be real brown sauce, with its sour malt vinegar bite. Barbecue sauce and steak sauce may be brown, but they are not brown sauce.

Pimm's and Lemonade

The basic ingredient of a great British summer is Pimm's No. 1 Cup, a fabulously fresh and fruity cocktail of gin, citrus and spice. Cricket, rain and turning pink in a deckchair on a pebble-strewn beach are all optional extras. Pimm's is the essential element of the season.

The drink's inventor was James Pimm, who ran an oyster bar in London and created the drink to help keep his customers' stomachs settled – a necessary concern when oysters are involved. Somehow it must have had the desired effect, as both Pimm's the drink and Pimm's Oyster Houses soon spread across the city.

Thankfully, there is a better way to serve Pimm's than with oysters, and that's the traditional long lemonade drink enjoyed by so many punters on the river Cam. The back of the bottle itself suggests one part Pimm's to three parts lemonade and an ample garnish of orange, mint, cucumber, strawberries, apples and lemon. I'd further suggest that it should always be mixed in a jug, not in a glass, and that splitting the lemonade with ginger ale gives it an extra spicy kick. Also, the drink should always be allowed to stand before serving so that the flavours of the fruit infuse the mixture – especially the cucumber, which adds a wonderful freshness. The result is an exceptionally refreshing drink that is dangerously easy to quaff – and once you have done drinking, you are left with a strange iced salad that you can rudely pick at from the jug.

No. 1 Cup was named after the tankard it was originally served in, not because there were any other cups in the sequence – but Pimm saw an opportunity and created successors, replacing the gin with whisky for a No. 2 Cup, brandy for No. 3, rum for No. 4, rye for No. 5 and vodka for No. 6. Most did not catch on, but No. 6 is still available if you know where to look, and No. 3 was recently rebranded as Winter Cup, to be served warm as a toddy, so that you can keep drinking Pimm's all through the year.

Scone

I've forgiven the Americans for misrepresenting the flapjack, since they do have a decent excuse (which is to say, they are in the right, curse them), but I shan't ever forgive them for what they've done to the scone. In the USA they have taken the basic idea of the scone – a small leavened bread that can be either sweet or savoury – and renamed it 'biscuit'. It is perhaps the most heretical act of cultural piracy ever committed. It would be akin to the British misappropriating jazz but choosing to refer to it as baseball. Wars have been fought over less!

The scone (rhymes with 'gone') is a wondrously versatile piece of baking ingenuity. Not only can you put almost anything on it, you can also bake almost anything into it. Fruit scone? Absolutely. Cheese scone? No problem. Chocolate? Potato? Ginger? Bacon? Honey? Nuts? Marijuana? Well, why the heck not! Versatility, thy name is scone. And scone, thy name is most certainly not biscuit.

The best thing to do with it, of course, is to serve it as a cream tea, with clotted cream and jam. This leads to some dissension between those who put the cream on first and those who put the jam on first. I have tried it both ways and found that I am far too euphorically happy at that precise moment to really care if there is any difference.

American biscuits are not served with cream and jam. They are served with a horrific meat dripping that looks as if it should be wiped up by a nurse. I think it is safe to say they have lost that culture war.

Trifle

I am fully prepared to admit that I am a fan of cake, especially a moist and airy sponge. I am also an ardent admirer of jelly, with its wanton wobble and jammy delectability. I am quite besotted with rich, thick cream, and I am easily seduced by cold, sweet custard. I even have time in my life for a few impudently tasty fruits and berries, and I have an ongoing and committed fondness for the occasional splash of booze.

The stars must have been in special alignment all those many years ago when some smart soul devised a dish that combines all these wonderful things into one gorgeous gaudy carnival of a dessert. It is a great irony that this cunning chef's substantial creation somehow earned the diminuitive name 'trifle', suggesting something slight. There is surely no such thing as a trifling trifle. Every trifle is important in the grand scheme of things, albeit in ways that we cannot hope to fully understand.

Trifle recipes vary greatly, but I am a trifle fundamentalist, and I won't accept anything calling itself trifle that does not have a layer of sponge infused with fruit juice and booze (sherry is traditional – rum is an excellent alternative), bejewelled with jelly-smothered fruit, then lavished with a thick layer of custard and topped with whipped peaks of beautiful cream. I can only shake my head with pity for anyone who uses a different trifle recipe. Their happiness has been trifled with.

FOR THE RECIPE SEE PAGE 215

Welsh Rarebit

Some people will tell you that Welsh rarebit is just a fancy name for cheese on toast. That's true in the same way that vodka is just a fancy name for mineral water.

No, cheese on toast is a dull and ordinary thing compared to Welsh rarebit. Cheese on toast is as simple as the name suggests – it is cheese on some toast. There is a little grilling involved, but that is really it.

Welsh rarebit is a much more sophisticated creation, which involves making a thick saucy batter of cheese, milk, mustard and beer. You spread this on toast and then you grill it. Fancy modern types might add Worcestershire sauce or even pickle. Thanks to the kick of the mustard and the earthiness of the beer, it is a snack that's altogether several magnitudes removed from the beige banality of boring old cheese on toast.

It is not clear whether Welsh rarebit actually originated in Wales, but the name certainly did not. In fact, the proper name is Welsh rabbit, and rarebit is just a corruption (but one that I happen to like the sound of), and it was applied by the English as a bit of an ethnic slur. The suggestion is that the Welsh are too poor to be able to afford rabbit, so they have to make do with this. Of course, I think the Welsh actually come out of the deal rather well. I think I'd much rather have a rarebit than a rabbit. Then again, rarebits make terrible pets.

FOR THE RECIPE SEE PAGE 214

Worcestershire Sauce

At one time I did not like anchovies at all, and I've only very recently come to appreciate their melting salty oiliness, even though they still look revolting. Back in the days when I was vehemently opposed to the idea of eating anchovies, I was shocked to discover that they are one of the key ingredients in Worcestershire sauce.

A brief crisis of faith followed. I do not eat anchovies, but I do eat Worcestershire sauce. Does this mean that I have to stop eating Worcestershire sauce? Then I realised that, regardless of how I felt about anchovies, I actually like Worcestershire sauce, so I should probably stop being such a bloody fool about it.

Worcestershire sauce is one of the world's great salt sauces, sitting alongside the soy sauce, the nam pla and the Tabasco sauce in any self-respecting foodie's cupboard. In addition to anchovies, it owes its unique character to a recipe that includes molasses, chilli peppers and more of those elusive tamarinds (see Brown Sauce, page 164). It is yet another British taste for which we should be thankful for our connections to India, as Worcestershire sauce was inspired by a recipe brought back from the subcontinent by a returning lord.

Worcestershire sauce is not really a vital ingredient in anything (except a Bloody Mary), yet it is a welcome addition to anything cheesy, meaty, or just in need of a bit of savoury pep. It is ideal in gravy or mince, or just for splashing on chips.

For those too terrified by the anchovies to dabble with Worcestershire sauce, there is an excellent vegetarian alternative produced in Sheffield – Henderson's Relish. It is inarguably very good, and the people of Sheffield swear that it is actually superior – but then, they would say that.

Sunday Roast

I suspect my family may have been among the last of a dying breed. Not only did we sit down around the dinner table together most evenings, away from the blare of the television, but we also had a full roast every Sunday, filling the hours between church and lunch by peeling potatoes and scoring sprouts. Apparently this sort of thing does not happen much any more. Even families who do eat together do so with their dinner on their knees in front of *Coronation Street*, while many modern couples rarely eat together at all because their schedules are so out of sync. Their children may be reared entirely on individually cooked ready-meals. Perhaps today's children already are.

It is a great shame because I think a good Sunday roast – or even a bad one – is the surest way to make a family feel connected. I miss those long, lazy Sundays a great deal, though I always used to resent the karmic trade-off that seemed to suggest that lunch was the reward for the tedium of church.

The perfect Sunday lunch is roast beef with red wine gravy (made with the juices from the roasting pan, of course), accompanied by roast potatoes, horseradish sauce, boiled carrots, sprouts and peas, and the pièce de résistance, Yorkshire pudding. Light, crispy, golden Yorkshires are a fine and noble institution, and I was going to include them on this list in their own right, but it would be an insult to take them away from the roast. Yorkshire pudding belongs on the Sunday plate, under a generous sheen of glistening meaty gravy. Yorkshire pudding alone is reason enough to bring back the Sunday roast. It might even be worth going to church and thanking God for.

FOR THE RECIPE SEE PAGE 213

Cheddar

In the unlikely event that aliens ever come to Earth and ask you to explain this thing humans call 'cheese' (presumably they would be aliens with a lot of spare time on their tentacles), odds are the first cheese you'll think of will be Cheddar. It is the definitive cheese, and the most popular cheese in the world. That buttery yellow Cheddar block is a food icon, and the taste of Cheddar can only best be described as, well, cheesy.

In fact, Cheddar means two things. It is both a generic and a specific cheese. In the generic sense, Cheddar refers to any cheese made in the Cheddar style, be it in America, Australia or Timbuktu. The cheddaring process involves squeezing the whey out of the curds to control the amount of moisture in the cheese, thus ensuring that it has the right texture and flavour.

In the specific sense, Cheddar is cheese made in this traditional style from traditional ingredients in its traditional setting – the West Country. Some would argue further that it has to be made near the town of Cheddar in Somerset, but that would limit real Cheddar to about three varieties.

The ubiquity of Cheddar is probably no bad thing. It is a fantastically versatile cheese, with varieties to suit just about every taste, but it is nice to know that the authentic variety is still out there, with its robust, nutty flavour and lively milky tang that buzzes in the mouth.

English Mustard

There are many different types of mustard in the world, each with a different balance of the same basic flavour, and each doubtless catering to the preferences of the local palate. I find German mustard too sour, while French mustard is very vinegary, and American mustard is far too sweet. All these mustards have their place, mind you. Well, except for the American. But I always like to have some wholegrain or Dijon mustard in the house because they're great for salad dressings. The rest of the time, the right mustard is always English, with its potent heat and fierce pungency.

The jar of English mustard in my cupboard sits right next to the French, but next to that is a tin of mustard powder, which is less convenient to spread on the edge of a plate, but it is the easiest way to add a tasty pinch of heat to Bolognese or gravy or cheese sauce.

It is also a great way to enjoy mustard at its liveliest. Here's the science bit: if you put a pinch of mustard powder in your mouth, you'll find it tastes almost entirely bland. When you mix it with cold water it sets off a chemical reaction, and it is only then that the familiar mustard heat develops. The flavour also fades over time, which is why you're better off always making your mustard fresh. Of course, if you can't stand the heat, get out of the kitchen – then pop down the shops and buy some terrible American mustard.

HobNobs

HobNobs are unique on this list, in being the only food stuff younger than me. Born in the 1980s, the HobNob is a young pretender at teatime – a prince among biscuits to the digestive's redoubtable king. Just this once, however, I am choosing impudent youth over venerable old age.

In the relatively short time that HobNobs have been on the market, they have established themselves as a fundamental part of British culture, doubtless equally beloved by students, grandmothers, cabbies, doctors, plumbers and princes. It is impossible to be presented with a plate of HobNobs to go with your mug of tea and not feel a little bit excited and spoilt. A HobNob is like a hug in biscuit form.

We could not have known it back in early 1985, but Britain had a HobNob-shaped hole in its heart back then, just waiting for a treacly baked oat biscuit that could fill it, thus bridging the gap between flapjacks and traditional dunking biscuits. Of course, if you really want to treat yourself, you could always invest in some chocolate HobNobs, where the chocolate will melt slightly in the tea and help hold the biscuit together in the dunk, but the classic plain HobNob should not be ignored in favour of its fancy brother.

Whichever HobNob you prefer, the old advertising slogan holds true: 'One nibble and you're nobbled'. Once opened, a packet of HobNobs will rarely find its way back to the cupboard.

Cadbury Dairy Milk

There's a lot of snobbery about chocolate. It seems that there are people in the world who think that chocolate should be bitter and taste of migraines. I am perfectly prepared to dabble in those fancy single-plantation, 70 per cent cocoa luxury chocolates, gussied up with lemon verbena oil or flecks of gold or essence of Bentley upholstery, but there is something extraordinarily tiresome about a chocolate that expects you to pander to it. Chocolate should be there at my indulgence, and not the other way around. We do not buy chocolate for its nutritional value, after all; we buy it so that we can gorge. You cannot gorge on chocolates that cost five quid for three.

In my view, chocolate and milk are one of the great flavour combinations, and chocolate does not get any better than this tuck shop classic, Cadbury Dairy Milk. It may not be classy – and some might say it is not even chocolate – but it gives me all the pleasure I want from my chocolate, and it is the best way to take a quick sugar hit.

Some European countries tried to ban British chocolate, or have it reclassified as 'family chocolate' because it contains vegetable fat, but to no avail. The European Court of Justice definitively ruled in 2003 that British chocolate is the real thing. In fact, I wouldn't care if it were made from the scrapings of a chip fryer and was only introduced once to a cocoa bean in passing. Cadbury Dairy Milk is better than the real thing. Anyway, let's face it: being snooty about chocolate makes about as much sense as being political about hopscotch.

Custard

The French call it crème anglaise (English cream) and I am never quite sure if that is meant to be a nod of appreciative recognition or a gesture of condescending disdain. Despite my better instincts, I am going to assume it is the former, because the French are clearly not immune to custard's charms. Like the British, they know it is good to have options when you are trying to decide what to pour over your bread and butter pudding or your rhubarb crumble.

These days it is actually getting increasingly difficult to buy proper custard, which should always include eggs. The first nail in the coffin of proper custard was Bird's easy-to-make, instant, egg-free pseudo-custard. The second nail may have been the now debunked idea that too many eggs are bad for cholesterol. And the final nail was surely the salmonella hysteria of the 1980s, which scared everyone away from undercooked eggs. As a consequence, my local supermarket stocks only one variety of egg custard, and that is from their snooty own-brand 'everything else we put our name to is inferior' range.

The answer to this dilemma, of course, is to make your own custard, which is much better anyway, and it is really not that hard to do. The only time you should ever buy pre-made custard is when it has been baked into a quiche, or in one of those lovely fresh custard tarts with their sweet soft pastry and creamy nutmeg hearts.

Marmalade

Marmalade is a bit of an international mongrel. The major ingredient is usually Spanish. It is a fruit preserve, which seems typically French. The name is essentially Portuguese. And the original recipe came from the Greeks via the Romans. It is the best argument I've ever heard for European integration.

Today we think of marmalade as being made of citrus fruit, but it is based on a Roman technique for preserving quinces, which was popularised by the Portuguese as *marmelado* (*marmelo* being Portuguese for 'quince'). It is possible that the Portuguese also adapted the technique for preserving oranges, but it was Scottish grocer James Keiller who, back in the eighteenth century, used the method to create a breakfast jelly filled with thick chunks of Seville orange peel, thus inventing Dundee marmalade with its delicious bittersweet tang.

You can also get marmalade without the bits in it, of course, but it is terribly dull stuff. Real marmalade shouldn't lie flat when you spread it – it should sit like a zesty Grand Canyon on your toast, every sticky morsel sending a buzz of flavour through your taste buds. Its bitterness makes it an ever so grown-up breakfast spread, and it goes so very well with a strong cup of tea or coffee. In my own personal nod towards European solidarity, I also think it is especially good on a hot buttered croissant.

Michael Bond – the creator of Paddington Bear, marmalade's most ardent fan – recently lamented that marmalade sales are on the wane because children want something sweeter. I can only hope that today's ungrateful brats grow up to be tomorrow's appreciative adults.

Clotted Cream

I have already praised the wondrousness of the scone, and now it is time to honour the other great ingredient in a classic cream tea: clotted cream. It merits its own mention because its uses go far beyond scones. It is the most wonderful accompaniment to sweet pies and puddings, and it turns even a lovely bowl of fresh, healthy fruit into an irresistible guilty pleasure. Even an ordinary slice of bread becomes decadent with a thick smear of clotted cream.

Cornish clotted cream already has the protected status that Melton Mowbray pork pies are chasing after, though Devon likes to claim that the cream actually originated there. Wherever it hails from, this rich, buttery cream is always made the same way – by slowly heating milk in shallow pans until it forms a beautiful golden crust. The result is a ludicrously heavy cream that's a heart-stopping 55 per cent fat or more – and you can taste every wonderful calorie.

When I die, I would like to be buried in clotted cream. In fact, that might well be the way that I do die.

Apples

The apple beats all the other fruit and veg in this list, and for good reason. The apple is the national fruit – a hardy, redoubtable and beautiful icon of Britishness.

The apple's traditional symbolic value is as the forbidden fruit that first tempted Eve, though it was more likely a fig or a pomegranate if it was meant to be anything at all, which is just as well, because surely no loving God could ever forbid the humble, decent apple?

Apples may have grown in Britain since prehistoric times, though those early wild apples were probably too sour to eat. It was under Roman occupation that Britain first cultivated apples, and that our famous apple orchards first took root. The orchards stumbled in the Middle Ages, though, with the Wars of the Roses trampling through the land, and it took a dedicated effort by Henry VIII to bring British apples back from the brink. The apple tree has been a symbol of the verdant British countryside ever since.

Apples are also a perpetual presence in British cooking, with the best apples having a tart bite that is ideal for pies or puddings or sausage or sauce – but, of course, they should also be enjoyed just as they are. An apple a day doesn't just keep the doctor away; it is also your patriotic duty. A lot of apples sold around the world come from former British colonies – New England, New Zealand and Australia – but the best are still British: sharp, robust Bramleys, rough, nutty Russets, and crisp, juicy Pippins. Apples are a national treasure.

Crumble

The single best thing to do to a Bramley apple – or, for that matter, to blackberries, gooseberries or rhubarb – is to turn them into crumble, the ultimate British pudding.

Crumble is a gloriously simple and simply glorious concept: sweetened stewed fruit baked beneath a crumbly biscuity top. It is so simple, and so good, that we should call back all our ambassadors and just send crumble to all the countries that we want to have good relations with. Golden, oozing hot crumble could be the end to all wars.

Crumble, to put it simply, tastes like home – and I do not mean that place you trudge back to after a long day at work so that you can pick up the bills from the doormat, stick a frozen meal in the microwave and collapse in front of a crappy evening soap. I mean home as in that familiar place where you and your loved one cosy up on the sofa in warmth and comfort, while a blustering wind whips at the house and a driving rain beats at the window, safe, satisfied and happy, with a tingle of blissful contentment creeping up from your toes to your smile. Crumble is domestic bliss in the form of a haphazard pie.

Now take all that and add generous lashings of thick, sweet custard or clotted cream and you'll know that Belinda Carlisle was right: heaven really is a place on Earth.

FOR THE RECIPE SEE PAGE 213

Full English Breakfast

The writer W. Somerset Maugham once quipped that the only way to eat well in England is to have breakfast three times a day. Obviously, I disagree or this list would have been a great deal shorter, but I take old Maughamy's point. The English breakfast is world-beating, and eating it three times in one day would certainly be a pleasure, though I am not sure it is possible. You would surely need a long rest after the first breakfast before you could tackle the second, and the third might remain but a distant dream. If I am ever forced to choose my method of execution, three English breakfasts a day might be the way I opt to go.

There's obviously no set formula for what makes up the perfect full English. Whenever I visit my local greasy spoon on a groggy, late Sunday morning, there is a moment of slow-dawning panic as I stare at the numbered breakfast options on the blackboard and wonder how to fit everything I want onto one plate. Bacon and eggs are surely the essential cornerstones, though how you want your eggs is a weighty question in itself. After that there is a choice of sausages, baked beans, black pudding, tomatoes, mushrooms, chips, sauté potatoes, fried slice, bubble and squeak, potato scones or toast. A mug of builder's tea with a teaspoon slowly dissolving within it is also a must.

Most of the classic components of a full English breakfast get their own entries in this list because they deserve to be celebrated in their own right. I suppose in a way that supports Maugham's case. The great British fry-up is a smorgasbord of the best of British food.

FOR THE RECIPE SEE PAGE 212

Bitter

There comes a time in every young British boy's life when he must decide what sort of a man he's going to be. Is he going to be a lager man, or is he going to be a bitter man? Generally, there will also come a time in adulthood when he realises that it is not an either/or choice, and it is possible to enjoy either one depending on mood, but for some reason during our late teenage years we become a little tribal about it.

I say that it is a choice, but I think it is usually predetermined by whatever a boy's father, elder brother or even friends are drinking. In my case, it was always inevitable that I would follow in my father's footsteps and be drawn to bitter. In fact, I was such a young crusty when it came to my choice of real ale that it became the deciding factor in my decision to go to university in Yorkshire. After all, university is just a three-year sabbatical from life, to be spent in pubs drinking beer.

I have since diversified my tastes to cover all kinds of beer, but my preference is still for a good pint of bitter. Whether hoppy or malty, fruity or nutty, earthy or coppery, bitter is always a welcome companion for a relaxed afternoon of pleasant conversation. It is a good idea to take a friend as well, though, because beer is not in itself a great conversationalist. At least, not until the sixth or seventh pint.

Sausages

I've often heard it said that no one would eat sausages if they knew what went in them. It is certainly true that the cheaper your sausage, the more fat, rind and gristle it is likely to contain, but good sausages are mostly belly pork and shoulder, perhaps with breadcrumbs and a little water to plump them out. That said, if a sausage tastes good enough, I would not really care if it was nothing but lips, tails and testicles, so long as I did not have to think too hard about it.

There are something like 400 varieties of sausage in Britain, with the most celebrated being the coarse, coiled Cumberland, the peppery Lincolnshire, the Gloucester Old Spot with sage, the West Country with apple, and the Welsh with leek. Then there are lamb, beef, game and boar sausages, or sausages flavoured with beer, garlic or whisky. You name it, and someone somewhere in Britain has tried to make a sausage out of it.

Britons spend over £500 million on almost 200,000 tonnes of sausage every year. We eat them in almost every household, and we enjoy them at every hour of the day, whether it is bangers at breakfast, a sausage sarnie for lunch, or a casserole or toad-in-the-hole at dinnertime. In the winter they're best with a big dish of fluffy, comforting mash, and in the summer they are ideal for roasting on the barbecue. When it comes to just sticking them in a pan, the instructions usually suggest a cooking time of about 15 minutes, but I prefer to fry my sausages for a good 40 minutes or more so that a nice thick, crispy black treacle forms around them. (I also usually cook more than I need so that I will have cold sausages to spare for breakfast the next morning. Cold, cooked sausages are a sublime pleasure.)

FOR THE RECIPE SEE PAGE 212

Marmite

Marmite is the single most contentious substance in the world – more so than crude oil, testosterone or antimatter. Indeed, some of my best friends hate Marmite, and like ideological fundamentalism, sociopathic tendencies or an affection for Jude Law, it is one of those seemingly insurmountable obstacles to friendship that I have manfully learnt to overlook.

Yet their aversion is still something that I will never understand. Marmite is nectar. Marmite is heaven. Marmite is dark, divine, thick, black, sticky distilled essence of paradise. People who do not like Marmite must be suffering some sort of deficiency of the soul. I suppose I should feel sorry for them. They cannot help the way they were made.

I do not think I could survive for long without Marmite. When I spent a summer in America I took the largest possible jar I could find with me rather than face a few months without, only to discover that American bread is not as dense as British bread and does not make the right kind of toast. I was excessively curmudgeonly for the rest of the summer. I can fully understand why British expatriates so often name Marmite as one of the things they miss most about home.

Marmite is actually made from a by-product of the beer-brewing process, which, according to my list, makes it the best thing ever to come out of a brewery. The yeasty paste was first identified by a German chemist, but apparently the Germans did not want it. Their loss is our gain.

Stilton

When I was a boy, the best thing one could hope for on a long drive up the motorway was a chance to stop off at a roadside eatery for an overpriced, greasy and unnervingly artificial-looking all-day breakfast. Back in those days it actually seemed like a treat. Maybe that was just because you always got a free lollipop on the way out.

Travellers on Britain's roads in the 1730s got a much better deal thanks to the efforts of Cooper Thornhill, a man who ought to be cheered as a great national hero. Cooper Thornhill was the genius who brought Stilton cheese to the world. He did not create it, but he did discover it in obscurity on a small Leicestershire farm, and decided that it was so good that he would start selling it at his pub, the Bell Inn, in the village of Stilton in Cambridgeshire, which sat on the busy Great North Road connecting London and York. From that moment on, Stilton's fame was assured. As a result, rather unusually, Stilton is never actually made in the place that it is named after, as it should be made only in Leicestershire, Derbyshire or Nottinghamshire.

There are several cheeses that pretend to the title of 'king of cheeses', and they are all excellent. The French have Brie de Meaux and Roquefort. The Italians have Parmigiano-Reggiano. Obviously, I have my bias, but I think the title undeniably belongs to Stilton – not just the best of Britain's 700 cheeses, but the greatest cheese in the world. According to a study by the British Cheese Board, it is the cheese most likely to give you surreal and vivid dreams. But Stilton, creamy, salty and utterly indulgent, is a dream all in itself.

Bacon

Vegetarianism, if such a thing truly exists, is a concept I simply cannot get to grips with. Vegetarians, if such creatures are not merely fanciful, must exist in some other dimension just slightly removed from our own, where the only difference between their world and ours is that their world never discovered bacon.

Bacon is without doubt the number one reason to eat meat. In fact, it is probably the number one reason to eat anything. The smell of frying bacon must be the human equivalent of catnip, making mouths water for miles around and sending passers-by into a frenzy of hunger. Bacon can even raise the dead, or near enough, being the single greatest cure for a hangover that man has ever been able to devise.

Whether it is fleshy, tender pink back bacon or ruddy, rippling streaky bacon, whether it is smoked or cured or just as nature intended, British bacon is world-class, succulent and delicious. It is best enjoyed with a fried breakfast or in a sandwich (with lots of brown sauce, of course), but there is probably no food in the world that would not benefit from a bit of bacon. It probably even tastes great in trifle. If God exists, he is surely made of British bacon.

Britain's dedication to bacon is so great that we even invented Canada so that we would have maple syrup to put on our bacon. That is love. I do not think that there has ever been a single moment of a single day of my life where I have not wanted to eat bacon.

Gin and Tonic

We can thank the Dutch for the invention of gin, which followed William of Orange to England during the Glorious Revolution (which I like to imagine is so called precisely because it brought gin to England). The original Dutch gin, or genever, was a rather rough sort of thing, resembling moonshine or potato vodka, and this was the sort of gin the peasants are seen ruining themselves with in the famous 1751 Hogarth print *Gin Lane*.

The sophisticated London dry gin that we know and love today emerged only after the invention of the column still in the 1830s, which transformed gin from a common, tawdry sort of drink into a smooth, sophisticated pleasure with a more fragrant botanical flavour.

However, gin would not find its perfect form until the Age of Empire, when Britons in tropical climates, forced to drink bitter quinine medicine to fend off malaria, decided to make the medicine a little more palatable by diluting it with gin. Over time the balance of gin and quinine shifted, to the point where the medicinal effects were probably negligible, but the cool reviving effects were all the more enjoyable.

In a sense, this most classic of drinks is really just a forebear to all those cough syrup-and-vodka mixes that students and underage drinkers keep trying to blind themselves with today. Modern gin and tonic will probably not protect you from malaria, but it may yet protect you from malaise. It is medicine for the soul.

The Cuppa

There could be only one winner in the contest for the greatest British contribution to world cuisine, and that is a good cup of tea, one of the most popular drinks in the world. Even though tea cannot actually be grown in Britain, the cuppa is undeniably a British achievement thanks to one very simple local variation: we add milk.

It seems the British have had a sense of the importance of tea from the moment we were first introduced to it because we decided that it was what our finest china was meant for. However, tea can only be made with fresh boiling water, and water that hot is no good for delicate cups, so some enterprising doyenne of the teapot decided to add a splash of cooling milk to the cup, and thus a national institution was born.

These days we drink tea out of robust ceramic mugs, but we still take it with milk. That, after all, is how it is meant to be. In most countries you have to specifically ask for it if you want milk in your tea, but in Britain you only speak up if you do not want milk.

Perhaps the best thing about tea is that it goes with absolutely everything, which explains how we are each able to consume roughly two and a half kilos of tea every year. You can drink it on its own, or with breakfast, lunch or dinner, or at mid-morning or mid-afternoon breaks or just before bed. It goes perfectly with sweet foods or savoury, and is just the ticket with spicy foods. It is a great refresher or a waker-upper, or you can use it to bring a little peace and calm into your life. It is an elixir, a comforter, a best friend and best beloved. Whether you live in Birmingham, Bolton, Brighton, Buxton, Bangor or Ballantrae, a cup of tea is what makes us all British. It is tea that brings meaning to our lives.

recipes

A lot of the food and drink in this book doesn't need a recipe. Everyone knows what to do with Marmite, for example, and it would be patronising to tell you how to eat your strawberries. You're not going to cultivate Maldon sea salt in your bath, you're probably not allowed to make Stilton in your guest bedroom, and no matter how good your kitchen is, you'll never make a Dairylea triangle.

However, if this book has helped you to work up an appetite, I wouldn't want to leave you without some advice on sating your hunger. The 35 recipes collected here will help you to prepare some of the trickier dishes in the book, including haggis, chicken tikka masala and the traditional Sunday roast, as well as giving you tips on some of those simple pleasures in life, such as Welsh rarebit and bubble and squeak. I hope you'll discover something new, or rediscover an old favourite. Enjoy, and eat well!

Note: All vegetables used in the recipes should be peeled unless stated otherwise. All spoon measures are level.

6 **Sausage Sandwich**
[Makes 2]

– oil for frying
– 4 plump English sausages
– butter
– 4 slices crusty white bread
– sauce of choice
– wholegrain mustard

1. Heat a little oil in a frying pan until hot. Add the sausages and fry over a medium heat until golden brown all over – at least 20 minutes, but longer if you like your sausages sticky and tarry.
2. Butter both sides of the bread. Cut the sausages in half lengthways and place on 2 slices of the bread.
3. Smother with brown sauce, ketchup or mustard, cover with the remaining bread and eat piping hot.

8 **Full English Breakfast**

There is no definitive way to serve a Full English Breakfast, so choose from the following options, cooked in the following order.

Sausages
Heat the frying pan, griddle pan or grill plate. Cook the sausages over a medium heat. They will need at least 20 minutes, so give them 10 minutes before you start cooking the rest of your breakfast, or cook them completely and keep them warm in the oven.

Bacon
Throw the bacon in next to the sausages and fry to your own preference – until pink and soft or brown and crispy. After cooking, place on some kitchen paper to soak up any excess fat.

Mushrooms
Clean off any dirt but do not wash. Cut in half and fry in a little olive oil for 5 minutes, stirring occasionally. Add a small knob of butter at the end of cooking for a nutty flavour.

Tomatoes
Cut the tomatoes in half. Season with salt and pepper and drizzle with a little olive oil. Place cut-side down under the

Eat Britain! 101 Great British Tastes

grill and cook for 2 minutes. Gently turn over and cook for a further 2–3 minutes.

Beans
Cook over a medium heat for about 5 minutes, stirring halfway through cooking.

Black Pudding
Remove the skin, if it has one, and fry for 2 minutes on each side until slightly crispy.

Eggs
Wipe the pan clean with kitchen paper, then heat 2 tablespoons of oil in it until hot. Lower the heat, then add the eggs and cook until just the way you like them.

For scrambled eggs, lightly beat the eggs in a bowl, add a little milk and butter and season to taste. Pour into a pan over a gentle heat and stir with a wooden spatula for about 2 minutes. Remove from the heat while still slightly runny, and add more butter to stop the eggs overcooking.

9 Rhubarb Crumble
[Serves 4]

– 15 sticks rhubarb, trimmed
– 4 tablespoons water
– 8 tablespoons caster sugar
– 1 teaspoon grated fresh root ginger
– zest 1 orange
– 180–200 g plain flour
– 110 g butter, softened
– 110 g demerara sugar
– 1 teaspoon cinnamon

1. Cut the rhubarb into finger-length pieces and place on a baking tray. Sprinkle with the water, dust with the sugar and roast for 10 minutes until jammy.
2. Transfer the rhubarb to an ovenproof dish and stir in the ginger and orange zest.
3. Preheat the oven to 180°C/350°F/gas mark 4.
4. To make the crumble topping, rub the flour and butter together until the mixture looks like breadcrumbs. Add the demerara sugar and cinnamon.
5. Smother the rhubarb with the crumble topping so that no rhubarb peeks through. Bake in the oven for 35–40 minutes. Leave to rest for 10–15 minutes before serving with vanilla ice cream, custard or cream.

18 Roast Beef and Yorkshire Puddings
[Serves 6]

– 1.75 kg organic rib of beef on the bone
– 4 heaped tablespoons English mustard
– 40 g butter
– 6 shallots
– 2 carrots, halved
– 1 garlic bulb, halved
– few sprigs fresh thyme

For the Roast Potatoes
– 900 g Maris Piper potatoes
– 225 g goose fat
– sea salt

For the Yorkshire Puddings
– 225 g plain flour
– 2 teaspoons English mustard powder
– 3 eggs, beaten
– 1 egg white
– 1 teaspoon fresh thyme leaves, or ½ teaspoon dried thyme
– 300–400 ml milk
– vegetable or groundnut oil

For the Gravy
– 1 heaped tablespoon plain flour
– ½ bottle full-bodied red wine
– 450 ml beef or vegetable stock
– sprigs fresh thyme
– freshly ground black pepper

Recipes

➤

1. Preheat oven to 220°C/425°F/gas mark 7.
2. Smear the beef with the lovely mustard, dot with the butter and place in the roasting tin. Toss the shallots, carrots, garlic and thyme in a little oil and scatter around the beef.
3. Put the tin in the oven and cook for 44 minutes per kilo. It should still be slightly pink in the middle.
4. Take the meat out of the oven and place on a warmed carving dish. Cover with foil and leave to rest for at least 15 minutes. Reserve the roasting pan with the juices and cooked vegetables for the gravy.
5. While the beef is cooking, cut the potatoes in half and par-boil for 6 minutes.
6. Drain and return to the pan. Cover with a lid and shake vigorously for a few seconds to make the potatoes fluffy at the edges.
7. Add the goose fat to a roasting tin and heat over a hob until smoking. Add the potatoes and fry for 5–8 minutes or until they are just starting to brown on all sides.
8. Transfer the roasting tin to the oven and cook for a further 60–90 minutes, or until crispy and golden brown on all sides. Remove from oven and sprinkle with sea salt.
9. To make the Yorkshire Puddings sift the flour, the mustard powder and a pinch of salt into a large bowl. Add the beaten eggs, egg white, thyme and enough milk to make a smooth, thick batter, about the consistency of double cream. Whisk well, then leave to stand for at least 30 minutes, or preferably overnight in the fridge.
10. Whisk the batter again just before using, adding extra milk if needed to return the batter to a double-cream consistency. Transfer to a jug.
11. Pour some oil into each hole of a 12-hole

cake tin. Place in the hot oven for a few minutes until the oil is almost smoking.
12. Carefully take out of the oven and pour the batter into the tin, almost filling each hole. Return to the oven and cook for 25–30 minutes, or until golden and crispy.
13. To make the gravy put the roasting tin containing the vegetables and meat juices over a medium heat. Vigorously stir in the flour, then pour in the wine and stock.
14. Add the thyme and bring to the boil, cooking for about 8–10 minutes until slightly thickened. Pour in any juices from the resting beef, then season with salt and pepper.
15. Strain through a sieve, pressing all the juices from the vegetables with the back of a wooden spoon. Serve piping hot in a pre-warmed jug.
16. Serve all the above with the vegetables of your choice. Just remember not to overboil them.

20 Welsh Rarebit
[Serves 2, but only if you are prepared to share]

– 25 g butter
– 25 g flour
– 150 ml beer (bitter, ale or porter)
– 1 teaspoon English mustard
– 2 teaspoons Worcestershire sauce
– 150 ml milk
– 175 g crumbly cheese:
  Caerphilly for the purists
– sea salt and freshly ground black pepper
– 4 slices thick bread

1. Melt the butter in a saucepan over a low heat. Slowly whisk in the flour and keep stirring for about 3 minutes, being careful not to let it brown.
2. Add the mustard, Worcestershire sauce and seasoning, whisking until smooth.
3. Slowly pour in the beer, again whisking until smooth.
4. Boil the milk in another pan, then slowly add to the flour mixture. Bring to the boil and, yes, keep whisking until smooth.
5. Crumble in the cheese. Keep whisking until – oh, you know.
6. Grill the bread on one side, then turn and spoon the cheese mixture onto the untoasted side. Return to the grill and cook until golden brown and bubbling.

For the spicier variation shown in the picture, spread some pickle or chutney on the untoasted surface before pouring on the cheese mixture. Alternatively, you could spread it with mustard, or even add a fried egg or a slice of ham, but that's a bit French.

21 Sherry and Raspberry Trifle
[Serves 6]

- 70g raspberry jam
- 225g plain sponge cake, sliced
- 150ml sherry
- 200g fresh raspberries
- 1 packet raspberry jelly
- 600ml milk
- 1 vanilla pod, split
- 50g caster sugar
- 6 egg yolks
- zest of 2 oranges
- 400ml double cream
- 25g toasted flaked almonds

1. Spread the jam over the slices of sponge cake and place in the bottom of a large glass dish.
2. Pour sherry over the cake and sprinkle fresh raspberries evenly over the top.
3. Dissolve the jelly in 300ml freshly boiled water, then add 300ml cold water and stir. Pour over the cake and raspberries and place in the fridge until set.
4. To make the custard, pour the milk into a pan, add the vanilla pod and bring to the boil.
5. In a separate bowl, mix the sugar and the egg yolks.
6. Once the milk is boiling, discard the vanilla pod and pour onto the egg mixture. Return to the pan, replace on the heat and stir the mixture until it coats the back of a wooden spoon. Do not allow to boil or it will curdle.
7. Pass the mixture through a sieve, add the orange zest and allow to cool. Pour over the jelly and sponge.
8. Whip the double cream and spread it over the custard.
9. Refrigerate the trifle for as long as possible, but preferably overnight. Just before serving sprinkle with the almonds or with hundreds and thousands or those little silver ball things if you are feeling especially retro.

28 Gressingham Duck with Sauté Potatoes and Grilled Chicory
[Serves 2]

– 450 g potatoes
– 3 tablespoons extra virgin olive oil
– small handful flatleaf parsley, chopped
– 2 breasts of Gressingham duck, about 175 g each
– 4 chicory heads
– 6 tablespoons sherry vinegar
– ½ garlic clove
– ½ teaspoon fresh thyme leaves
– sea salt and freshly ground black pepper

1. Par-boil the potatoes for 10 minutes. Drain and chop into chunks.
2. Heat 1 tablespoon olive oil in a heavy-based frying pan and toss in the potato. Fry until golden brown. Add some salt and the parsley.
3. While the potatoes are cooking, trim the duck breasts neatly and score the skin, taking care not to cut through the fat.
4. Heat 1 tablespoon oil in a non-stick frying pan and fry the duck breasts skin-side down for a few moments until crispy and brown. Fat will seep out. Tip this away so it does not burn. Turn the breasts and brown the flesh side. Season as they cook. Turn once more and baste the flesh side a few times with the pan juices. Duck is best served slightly pink and

juicy, so cook for a total of 8–10 minutes. Remove from the pan and keep warm.
5. To make the dressing put the sherry vinegar into a small pan and place over a medium heat until reduced to about 2 tablespoons. Crush the garlic and thyme with a pestle and mortar until you have a smooth paste. Add the reduced vinegar and season. Stir in 1 tablespoon olive oil and set aside.
6. Cut off the base of the chicory, keeping it intact and slice in half lengthways. Place the chicory on a hot griddle pan and cook until slightly charred on both sides.
7. To serve, slice the duck breasts into diagonals and place on a bed of chicory. Drizzle the dressing over the top and serve with the potatoes.

33 Sticky Toffee Pudding
[Serves 6]

– 85 g butter, softened
– 25 g plain flour
– 150 g dark Demerara sugar
– 175 g stoned dried dates
– 2 tablespoons dark rum
– 300 ml water
– 1 tablespoon golden syrup
– 2 tablespoons black treacle
– 2 eggs
– 1 teaspoon vanilla essence
– 200 g self-raising flour
– 1 tablespoon bicarbonate of soda

For the Sauce
– 100 ml double cream
– 40 g butter
– 40 g dark brown sugar
– 2 tablespoons black treacle
– 1 tablespoon golden syrup

1. Preheat the oven to 200°C/400°F/gas mark 6.
2. Take 25 g of the butter and use to grease a 12 cm pudding basin. Scatter the plain flour over the buttered surface to coat it thoroughly. Discard any excess flour.
3. Combine the remaining butter with the Demerara sugar in a mixing bowl.
4. Put the dates, rum and water in a small pan and bring to the boil.

5. Stir the golden syrup, black treacle, eggs and vanilla essence into the butter mixture, then slowly mix in the self-raising flour.

6. Blitz the hot rum and date mixture in a blender, add the bicarbonate of soda, then combine with the egg and butter mixture.

7. Pour the resulting gloop into the pudding basin and bake in the oven for 20–25 minutes, until the pudding is just firm to the touch.

8. To make the sauce, place the cream, butter, sugar, treacle and syrup in a pan, stir together and bring to the boil.

9. Run a knife around the edge of the pudding and invert onto a plate. Pour the sauce over it and serve.

37 **Chicken Tikka Masala**
[Serves 4]

– 4 chicken breasts, each
  cut into 4 - 6 pieces

Tikka Marinade
– 1 teaspoon fenugreek seeds
– 1 teaspoon caraway seeds
– 3 tablespoons garam masala
– 1 teaspoon chilli powder
– a handful fresh chopped coriander
– 6 tablespoons plain yoghurt
– 1 teaspoon crushed garlic
– 1 teaspoon grated ginger
– 1 teaspoon English mustard powder
– 1 teaspoon ground turmeric
– the juice of 1 lemon
– 3 tablespoons vegetable oil

Masala Sauce
– 150 g unroasted cashews
– 1 small carton double cream
– 800 g tinned chopped tomatoes
– 1 tablespoon tomato purée
– 4 teaspoons sugar
– 1 teaspoon sea salt
– 2 teaspoons cumin powder
– 1 teaspoon chilli powder
– 3 teaspoons garam masala
– large knob of butter
– small handful chopped coriander

1. Start by making the marinade. Crush the

fenugreek and caraway seeds using a pestle and mortar, then transfer to a mixing bowl.

2. Stir the remaining marinade ingredients together in a bowl, toss in the chicken then cover and leave in the fridge for 1 hour.

3. Preheat the oven to 250°C/482°F/gas mark 9.

4. To make the sauce blitz the cashews in a blender. Add 200 ml of the cream and blitz again to create a rough paste.

5. Put the paste in a pan with the tomatoes, tomato purée, sugar, salt, cumin, chilli and garam masala. Simmer, stirring regularly, for 25 minutes, adding a little water if the mixture becomes too thick.

6. Place the chicken pieces in a baking dish, pour over the marinade and cook in the oven for 15 minutes, until golden.

7. Add the chicken to the sauce on the hob and stir in the butter, the remaining cream and the chopped coriander. Taste and season with salt or extra chilli if desired.

8. Garnish with more fresh coriander and serve with rice and naan bread.

39 Porridge
[Serves 2]

– 4 tablespoons medium porridge oats
– 450 ml water
– 150 ml full-fat milk
– ½ teaspoon sea salt
– 1 tablespoon cream

1. Place the oats, salt, water and milk in a medium saucepan and bring to the boil.
2. Reduce to a simmer and stir continuously for 10–15 minutes, until thickened.
3. Take off the heat, add the cream and stir well.
4. Serve with sugar, salt, jam, golden syrup or whatever you prefer.

40 Flapjack
[Makes 10]

– 75 g butter
– 75 g light brown sugar
– 1 tablespoon golden syrup
– 175 g porridge oats

1. Preheat the oven to 180°C/350°F/gas mark 4. Grease a shallow baking tin (about 18cm square) with a little butter.
2. Place the butter, sugar and syrup in a saucepan and stir over a low heat until the butter and sugar have melted. Add the oats and stir thoroughly.
3. Press the mixture into the prepared tin and bake in the centre of the oven for 25 minutes, or until evenly golden brown.
4. Mark into equal slices while still warm, but allow to cool in the tin before removing. No, seriously; be patient.

43 Fish and Chips
[Serves 4]

– beef dripping or vegetable oil, for deep frying
– 6 - 8 large, floury potatoes (Maris Piper or King Edwards)
– 4 x 175 g thick white-fish fillets
– sea salt and freshly ground black pepper
– flour, for dusting

For the Batter
– 225 g self-raising flour
– 300 ml cold lager

For the Tartare Sauce
– 250 ml mayonnaise
– 2 teaspoons lemon zest
– 1 tablespoon lemon juice
– 2 tablespoons finely chopped gherkins
– 2 tablespoons finely chopped capers
– 1 tablespoon chopped fresh dill

1. Put the dripping or oil in a deep fat fryer or a deep saucepan and heat to 120°C / 250°F.
2. Start by making the chips. Cut the potatoes into chunky slices. Wash well in cold water, drain and pat dry with kitchen paper. Put the potatoes into the hot oil and fry gently for about 8–10 minutes, until they are soft but still pale. Check that they are cooked by piercing with a small,

sharp knife. Lift out of the pan and leave to cool slightly on greaseproof paper.

3. Increase the heat of the oil to 180°C/350°F.

4. Season the fish and dust lightly with flour.

5. Preheat the oven to 150°C/300°F/gas mark 2.

6. To make the batter, sift the flour and a pinch of salt into a large bowl and whisk in the lager. The mixture should be the consistency of very thick double cream and should coat the back of a wooden spoon.

7. Dip 2 of the fillets in the batter, then carefully lower in the hot fat. Cook for 8–10 minutes, until golden and crispy.

8. Remove the fish from the pan, drain on kitchen paper, then place on a baking sheet lined with greaseproof paper. Keep warm in the oven while you cook the remaining 2 fillets in the same way.

9. Once the fish is cooked, return the chips to the hot oil and cook for 2–3 minutes, or until golden and crispy.

10. Meanwhile, make the tartare sauce by simply mixing all the ingredients together in a bowl.

11. Shake any excess oil off the chips and season with salt before serving with the crispy fish and tartare sauce.

44 Shepherd's Pie
[Serves 4]

- olive oil, for frying
- 450 g minced lamb
- 1 large onion, chopped
- 1 bay leaf
- 2 carrots, diced
- 25 g plain flour
- 300 ml lamb or beef stock
- sea salt and freshly ground black pepper
- 1 tablespoon sun-dried tomato purée
- 700 g potatoes, quartered
- 25 g butter
- 4 tablespoons milk
- 50 g Cheddar cheese (optional)

1. Preheat the oven to 200°C/400°F/gas mark 6.

2. Heat a little olive oil in a frying pan and fry the lamb with the onion, bay leaf and carrots for 8–10 minutes.

3. Add the flour and stir for a couple of minutes. Slowly add the stock, then stir in the tomato purée. Bring to the boil, add seasoning, then cover and simmer gently for 25 minutes.

4. Meanwhile, cook the potatoes in boiling salted water for 20 minutes, until tender. Drain well, mash with the butter and milk, and set aside.

5. Remove the bay leaf from the mince and place the mixture in a large ovenproof dish.

6. Spread the potato on top of the mince. Sprinkle the grated cheese over the top if you wish, and bake for 15-20 minutes.

7. Serve hot with a vegtable on the side. I recommend peas, which mush up nicely with the pie.

47 **Bread Pudding**
[Serves 6]

- 225 g stale bread, torn into chunks
- 110 g currants, raisins or sultanas
- 50 g brown sugar
- 50 g butter, melted
- ½ teaspoon mixed spice
- ½ teaspoon cinnamon
- 1 egg
- about 500 ml milk

1. Pre-heat the oven to 170°C/325°F/gas mark 3.

2. Soak the bread in cold water for about 1 hour, then squeeze dry.

3. Mush up the bread with the dried fruit, sugar, butter and spices.

4. Add the egg and milk, and mix well.

5. Pour the mixture into a small greased loaf tin and bake for about 1 hour, until firm to the touch.

6. Sprinkle with a little extra sugar and cinnamon, and serve hot with custard.

Recipes

219

48 **Crusted Roast Fillet of Aberdeen Angus Beef**
[Serves 4]

— 600 g Aberdeen Angus beef fillet
— 30 g porridge oats
— 1 tablespoon black peppercorns, crushed
— zest of 1 unwaxed lemon
— sea salt
— 1 teaspoon butter
— 150 ml beef stock
— 150 ml double cream
— 1 tablespoon lemon juice

1. Preheat the oven to 220°C/425°F/gas mark 7.
2. Place a small, lightly buttered roasting tin in the oven.
3. Mix the oats, peppercorns and lemon zest in a bowl with a little salt. Roll the fillet in the mixture until thickly coated, leaving the ends bare. Dot with the butter and place in the hot tin.
4. Roast for 15 minutes. Turn off the heat, transfer the fillet to a carving plate, cover with foil and return to the oven to rest, leaving the door ajar.
5. Place the roasting tin on the hob. Pour in the beef stock and bring to the boil, scraping up all the roasting residues. Reduce the liquid by half then add the cream and boil until thick. Stir in the lemon juice and pour into a warm jug or bowl.
6. Carve the fillet into thick slices.

Serve with dauphinoise potatoes, green beans and the cream sauce.

49 **Fruit Fool**
[Serves 2]

— 100 g fresh strawberries, quartered
— 100 g fresh raspberries
— 50 g fresh blueberries
— juice of ½ lemon
— 2 tablespoons icing sugar, sifted
— 1 small carton double cream
— sprigs of mint, plus a few fresh berries for garnish

1. Mash or blend together 75 g each of the strawberries and raspberries. Mash in half the blueberries with the lemon juice and sugar.
2. In a medium bowl, whip the cream to soft peaks.
3. Fold half the mashed fruit into the cream to create marble ripples.
4. In a small bowl, gently mix the whole berries with the rest of the mashed fruit.
5. Serve by spooning alternating dollops of the fruit and the cream mixture into dishes. Just don't be too dainty about it. Garnish with a mint sprig for that real 1970's retro look.

50 **Scotch Broth**
[Serves 6]

— 454 g neck of mutton or lamb
— 25 g pearl barley
— 1.4 litres of water
— 1 small turnip, chopped
— 1 leek, chopped
— 1 large carrot, chopped
— 1 small carrot, grated
— 1 onion, chopped
— 25 g cabbage, shredded
— sea salt and freshly ground black pepper
— chopped parsley, to garnish

1. Place the meat, pearl barley and water in a saucepan. Bring to the boil, then cover and simmer for 1 hour, skimming off any white scum.
2. Add the turnip, leek, chopped carrot and onion. Cover and simmer for 30 minutes.
3. Add the grated carrot and the cabbage, season and simmer for a further 30 minutes.
4. Before serving, take the meat off the bones and return it to the broth. Discard the bones.
5. Bring back to the boil and serve, garnished with chopped parsley.

52 Pie and Mash
[Serves 4]

- 2 tablespoons vegetable oil
- 600 g Aberdeen Angus minced beef
- 1 medium onion, chopped
- 2 garlic cloves, crushed
- 2 tablespoons plain flour
- 2 tablespoons sundried tomato purée
- 1 teaspoon English mustard
- 75 g mushrooms, finely chopped
- 300 ml brown ale or bitter
- sea salt and freshly ground black pepper
- 400 g shop-bought puff pastry
- milk, to glaze

For the Mash
- 6 large Maris Piper potatoes (about 1.5 kg)
- 150 ml full-fat milk
- 100 g unsalted butter
- 2 tablespoons olive oil

For the Parsley Liquor
- 100 g frozen peas
- 300 ml potato, skimmed
- large handful of fresh curly parsley
- 1 teaspoon cornflour
- 1 teaspoon white vinegar

1. Heat the oil in a frying pan, add the beef and fry for 2 minutes, until brown. Add the onion and garlic and fry for a further 2 minutes. Stir in the flour and tomato

purée and cook for another 2 minutes
2. Add the mustard, mushrooms and brown ale and bring slowly to the boil. Season, then cover and simmer for 20 minutes. Remove from heat and allow to cool.
3. Turn the beef mixture into a 1-litre pie dish or 4 individual pie dishes.
4. Preheat the oven to 220°C/425°F/gas mark 7.
5. Flour a work surface and roll out the pastry enough to cover the pie dish(es). Place the pastry over the meat and trim off the excess. Press the edges down firmly. Get out a few pastry shapes to decorate the top if you wish. Brush the pastry with milk to glaze.
6. Place the pie in the oven for 20–25 minutes (15 minutes for individual pies), or until golden brown.
7. While the pie is baking, cut the potatoes in half and boil in a pan of salted water for about 20 minutes. Test for readiness by piercing with a knife.
8. Drain the potatoes, reserving the water for the parsley liquor.
9. Return the potatoes to the pan and shake over a low heat for 30 seconds to dry them off.
10. Remove from the heat and mash well.
11. Warm the milk in a pan, then pour onto the potatoes. Add the butter and olive oil, and mix well. Season with salt and pepper
12. Put the peas, water and most of the parsley into a blender and whizz together.
13. Sieve the liquid into a saucepan and add the remaining parsley, finely chopped (about 2-3 tablespoons). Bring to the boil.
14. Mix the cornflour with a little cold water and add to the sauce, stirring constantly.
15. Add the vinegar and season to taste.

54 Treacle Tart
[Serves 6]

- 170 g brown breadcrumbs (about ½ large loaf)
- 200 g unsalted butter
- 3 large eggs
- 75 ml double cream
- 2 teaspoons sea salt
- 900 g golden syrup
- zest of 3 lemons
- juice of 2 lemons

For the pastry
- 400 g plain flour
- 1 heaped teaspoon sea salt
- 400 g unsalted butter, chilled and diced
- 100 g icing sugar
- zest of 1 lemon, finely grated
- seeds from 1 vanilla pod
- 2 large egg yolks
- 2 large eggs

1. First make the pastry. Place the flour and salt in a large bowl, add the butter and rub together until the mixture resembles breadcrumbs.
2. Stir in the icing sugar, lemon zest and vanilla seeds. Add the egg yolks and the eggs, and mix to make a dough. Wrap the dough in clingfilm and leave it to rest in the fridge for at least 3 hours.
3. Preheat the oven to 200°C/400°F/gas mark 6. ➤

4. Lightly butter and flour a flan tin.
5. Take the pastry out of the fridge and place two-thirds of it between two sheets of greaseproof paper. Roll out until you have a circle 3–5 mm thick and 45–50 cm across.
6. Peel off the top sheet of greaseproof paper and roll the dough onto the rolling pin, removing the bottom sheet of paper as you go. Unroll the pastry over the prepared flan tin and gently push it into the base and sides. Chill for 30 minutes
7. Remove the pastry case from the fridge and prick the base with a fork. Place a fresh piece of greaseproof paper, cut to size, over the pastry base. Put ceramic beans or rice on top, and bake blind in the oven for 12–15 minutes. Remove the beans and greaseproof paper then return the pastry case to the oven for 5 minutes to dry out.
8. To make the breadcrumbs, discard the crusts and blitz the soft parts in a food processor.
9. Put the butter in a sauce pan over a medium heat. When it stops sizzling and develops a nutty aroma, take off the heat, strain it into a bowl and leave to cool.
10. Put the eggs, cream and salt into a bowl and whisk until combined.
11. Pour the golden syrup into a pan and heat gently until liquid. Pour 115 g of the butter into the warmed syrup and stir well.
12. Pour the buttery syrup into the egg and cream mixture. Stir in the breadcrumbs with the lemon zest and juice, and pour the mixture into the pastry case.
13. Roll out the remaining pastry and cut into stips about 1 cm wide. Arrange them on top of the tart in a lattice-work effect.
14. Place the tart in the oven and bake for 30–40 minutes, or until it is a deep-brown colour. Allow to cool before taking out of the tin.
15. Serve with big dollops of a good vanilla ice cream.

58 Toad-in-the-hole
[Serves 4]

— 75 g butter
— 2 or 3 large onions, thinly sliced
— 1 or 2 red onions, thinly sliced
— 1 tablespoon groundnut oil
— 450 g pork sausages
— 400 ml chicken or beef stock
— 100 ml Madeira
— 2 teaspoons mustard
— 1 teaspoon Worcestershire sauce
— sea salt and freshly ground black pepper
— sprigs of rosemary

For the Batter
— 110 g plain flour
— 2 eggs
— 300 ml semi-skimmed milk

1. Melt the butter in a heavy based pan and gently fry the onion, for 20 minutes, stirring frequently until soft.
2. Turn the heat down low and continue cooking the onions until brown – this should take about an hour.
3. Meanwhile, make the batter. Sift the flour and salt into a large wide bowl. Make a well in the centre of the flour and break both eggs into it. Mix with a wooden spoon, then gradually add the milk. You should end up with a thin paste.
4. Leave the batter to stand for at least

30 minutes at room temperature. Meanwhile, preheat the oven to 220°C/425°F/gas mark 7.

5. Add half the oil to a frying pan and cook the sausages until evenly browned all over, but do not cook them through.

6. Add the stock, Madeira, mustard, Worcestershire sauce and seasoning to the onions. Bring this gravy to a simmer, stirring frequently.

7. Heat the rest of the oil in a shallow ovenproof dish or roasting tin until it starts to smoke. Add the sausages to it and pour the batter around (but not over) the sausages. Sprinkle with the sprigs of rosemary.

8. Bake until the batter is risen and golden. This should take around 30 minutes, but may vary, depending on the depth of the batter.

9. Serve with the hot onion gravy.

62 Welsh Lamb with Apricot and Pistachio Stuffing

[Serves 6]

- 2 tablespoons fresh rosemary, finely chopped
- 2 tablespoons finely chopped apricots
- 2 garlic cloves, crushed
- 2 tablespoons finely chopped pistachio nuts
- 1 teaspoon ground cumin
- olive oil
- 1.5–2 kg shoulder of spring Welsh lamb
- 300 ml cider
- 1 onion, quartered
- 1 carrot, chopped
- honey
- sea salt and freshly ground black pepper

1. In a bowl mix the rosemary, apricots, garlic, pistachio nuts and cumin with a little olive oil. Season with salt and pepper.

2. Pierce the lamb in several places with a thin, sharp knife. Use your fingers to push the stuffing into the incisions.

3. Put the lamb in a roasting tin and pour the cider around it. Toss in the onion and carrot, and roast in the oven at 200°C/400°F/gas mark 6 for 30 minutes.

4. Lower the heat to 160°C/320°F/gas mark 3, and cook for a further 75 minutes. Baste frequently while cooking, adding a little more cider if it appears to be drying up.

5. Transfer the cooked joint to a warmed serving plate, cover with foil and leave to rest for 10 minutes before carving.

6. Pour off any excess fat from the roasting tin and reduce the remaining liquid slightly by heating on top of the stove. Mash the onion and carrot into the liquid. Add a tablespoon of honey and more cider if necessary. Sieve the gravy and pour into a warmed jug.

7. Serve the lamb with roast potatoes, green beans and baby carrots.

63 **Lamb Balti**

[Serves 6]

- 900 g lamb, cut into 2-5 cm cubes
- 275 ml water
- 2 tablespoons minced garlic
- 120 g ghee (clarified butter)
- 225 g grated onions
- 1 tablespoon ground coriander
- 2 tablespoons ground cumin
- ¼ teaspoon ground clove
- ½ teaspoon ground cinnamon
- 1 teaspoon ground cardamom
- ¼ teaspoon dried thyme
- ½ teaspoon ground fennel seed
- 2 teaspoons hot mustard powder
- ¼ teaspoon ground fenugreek seed
- ½ teaspoon dried fenugreek leaf
- ¼ teaspoon dried curry leaf
- ¼ teaspoon black onion seeds
- 1 teaspoon cayenne pepper
- 175 g tomato purée
- ¾ teaspoon sea salt
- bunch fresh chopped coriander

1. Rinse the lamb and add to a heavy pan with the water and garlic. Bring to the boil, then simmer with the lid on until tender – about 45 minutes. When done, turn off the heat and leave to stand for 20 minutes.
2. Melt the ghee in a large heavy pan. Add the onions and fry until just starting to brown. Add all the herbs and spices and fry for 2–3 minutes.
3. Add the tomato purée and salt. Fry until most of the liquid has gone – it should look like a thick brown gravy.
4. Drain the lamb and add to the gravy. Continue frying for another 5–10 minutes, or until the dish is almost dry. Remove from the heat. Garnish with fresh coriander and serve with plenty of naan bread, chapattis or parathas.

65 **Ploughman's Lunch**

[Serves 2]

Bare Essentials
- crusty wholemeal bread
- cheese, such as Cheddar, Double Gloucester or Stilton, or a little of each
- pickle or chutney, the spicier and fruitier the better

Optional Extras
- 1 crisp apple, cut in half (Cox's or Russetts are particularly good, as their tart flavour cuts through the cheese)
- 1 or 2 pickled onions
- mixed salad leaves, with grated carrot and celery
- a few slices of thick-cut ham, off the bone

Arrange the ingredients on a plate and serve with a pint of scrumpy cider or frothy ale for a perfect pub-style lunch.

70 **Wild Scottish Smoked Salmon**

[Serves 2]

– wild Scottish smoked
  salmon, lightly sliced
– brown bread, cut into medium slices
– butter
– 1 lemon
– freshly ground black pepper

1. Butter the bread and cut in half diagonally.
2. Drape a generous amount of smoked salmon over each slice of bread.
3. Season with a twist of black pepper and a squeeze of lemon juice.
4. Serve with champagne, prosecco or cava.

71 **Cornish Pasty**

[Makes 4]

– 50 g chopped onion or shallot
– 50–75 g diced turnip or swede
– 100 g beef steak, cut into 1 cm cubes
– 150 g diced potatoes, placed in cold water
– sea salt and freshly ground black pepper
– beaten egg or milk, to glaze

For the Pastry
– 450 g strong white flour
– 100 g lard
– 100 g butter
– 175 ml water

1. First make the pastry. Put the flour and a little salt into a bowl. Add 25 g of the lard and rub into the flour.
2. Slice the rest of the lard and the butter into the mixture and stir with a knife. Add all the water and stir until absorbed.
3. Knead the mixture on a floured surface for a couple of minutes, then cover and leave in the fridge for at least 30 minutes.
4. Cut the pastry into 4 equal pieces. Flour a work surface and roll out each piece into a circle about 22 cm in diameter. Place an upturned plate of similar diameter on the pastry and trim around it.
5. Preheat the oven to 220°C/425°F/gas mark 7.
6. Put a little of the onion, turnip and potato in the centre of each pastry circle. Season with salt and pepper.
7. Scatter the meat on top and around the vegetables. Sprinkle with salt.
8. Top the meat with the remaining vegetables and add more salt.
9. Dampen the edge of the pastry with a little water and fold over to form semi-circle. Seal the pasties by pressing firmly around the edge. Fold the edge inwards and press down again, crimping all along it with your forefinger and thumb. Make sure the pasties are fully sealed.
10. Use a sharp knife to make a slit in the upper side of each pasty. Place on buttered greaseproof paper and brush with beaten egg or milk.
11. Bake in the oven for 20–30 minutes. Turn off the heat after 15 minutes, but leave the pasties inside with the door shut.
12. Remove from oven and place on a wire rack for 15 minutes to cool.

75 **Bubble and Squeak**
[Serves 4]

– 450 g leftover cooked potatoes
– 225 g leftover cooked cabbage,
  sprouts or other greens
– 25 g butter or oil
– 4 spring onions or 2 leeks,
  roughly chopped
– sea salt and freshly ground black pepper

Method
1. Heat the butter in a large frying pan.
2. Add the white parts of the spring onions
and cook until soft and transparent.
3. Add the potatoes, cabbage and
green tops of the spring onions.
Mix well and season to taste.
4. Fry the mixture over a medium
heat, turning occasionally, until the
potato is golden brown and crispy.

79 **Fried Slice**
[Serves 1]

– 1–2 tablespoons vegetable oil
– thick sliced white bread
  preferably 2 days old
– butter

1. Heat the oil in a frying pan.
2. Add the bread and fry for 2–3 minutes
on one side, until crispy and golden.
3. Add a knob of butter and turn the slice.
Fry this side until crisp and golden too.
4. Serve with a cooked breakfast,
or at least a hot cup of tea.

80 **Marmalade Bread and Butter Pudding**
[Serves 4]

– 30 g unsalted butter
– 50 g sultanas
– 2 tablespoons dark rum
– 6 medium slices white bread,
  crusts removed
– Seville orange marmalade
– 2 eggs
– 2 egg yolks
– 3 tablespoons caster sugar
– 150 ml milk
– 300 ml double cream
– vanilla essence
– 1 teaspoon ground cinnamon
– 2 tablespoons demerara sugar

1. Grease a 1.5-litre pudding dish
with some of the butter.
2. Put the sultanas in a bowl with the rum
and microwave on full power for 1 minute.
3. Spread both sides of the bread with
the butter and marmalade, and cut into
triangles. Arrange them evenly along
the middle of the pudding dish.
4. Sprinkle the rum-soaked
sultanas over the bread.
5. Put the eggs, egg yolks, caster
sugar, milk, cream and vanilla essence
in a bowl and whisk together.
6. Pour this mixture over the bread

and leave to soak for 20 minutes.

7. Preheat the oven to 180°C/350°F/gas mark 4.

8. Sprinkle the pudding with the cinnamon and demerara sugar. Place in a roasting tin of hot water and cook in the middle of the oven for 45 minutes, or until the egg mixture sets and the top has browned.

9. Remove from the oven and leave to stand for 10 minutes.

10. Serve with custard, cream or good-quality vanilla ice cream.

83 Queen of Puddings
[Serves 4]

– 600 ml milk
– 1 teaspoon vanilla extract
– 15 g butter
– 100 g fresh white breadcrumbs
– 210 g caster sugar
– salt
– grated rind of 1 lemon
– 2 eggs, separated
– 3 or 4 level tablespoons of raspberry or other berry jam

1. Pour the milk and vanilla extract into a saucepan and bring to the boil. Remove from the heat and stir in the butter, breadcrumbs, 25 g of sugar, a pinch of salt and the lemon rind. Set aside for 20 minutes.

2. Preheat the oven to 180°C/350°F/gas mark 4 and generously butter a 1-litre pie dish.

3. Beat the egg yolks and add to the cooled bread mixture.

4. Spread the mixture evenly into the prepared dish and bake in the centre of the oven for about 30 minutes, or until set.

5. When the pudding is cooked, place the jam in a small saucepan and melt over a low heat. Spread the jam in a thin even layer over the top of the pudding.

6. Beat the egg whites into soft mounds. Gradually add most of the rest of the sugar, beating until stiff. Spread this meringue

mixture on top of the jam, and sprinkle with the remaining pinches of sugar.

7. Bake for 10–15 minutes, until the meringue is golden brown. Serve cold or at room temperature.

85 Apple Sauce
[Serves 4 - 6]

– 450 g cooking apples, peeled, cored and roughly chopped
– 50 ml dry cider
– 25 g caster sugar
– 50 g unsalted butter
– freshly ground black pepper
– ½ teaspoon ground cinnamon

1. Put the apples in a saucepan with the cider, sugar and butter and cook over a low heat until the apples have broken down into a purée. This should take about 15 minutes.

2. Season with a little pepper and the cinnamon. Pass the mixture through a sieve or whizz in a blender.

3. Reheat and serve with roast pork and all the trimmings.

Recipes

86 **Cucumber Sandwiches**
[Makes 16 - 20 quarters]

– butter
– 8 - 10 thin slices of bread
– 1 cucumber, peeled and thinly sliced
– sea salt

1. Butter the bread and arrange
the cucumber on half the slices.
Season generously with salt and
top with the remaining bread.
2. Trim off the crusts and cut the
sandwiches into quarters.

92 **Beer-battered Scampi**
[Serves 4]

– 275 g plain flour, sifted
– sea salt and freshly ground black pepper
– 1 egg
– 1 tablespoon sunflower oil
– 275 ml beer
– vegetable oil, for deep frying
– 32 raw scampi, shells removed

1. Put 225g of the flour in a bowl
and mix in some seasoning. Make a
well in the centre, add the egg and
sunflower oil, whisk together.
2. Slowly whisk in the beer to make a thick
batter. Leave to rest for at least 30 minutes.
3. Heat the vegetable oil to about
180°C/350°F. Put 50g flour on a
shallow plate near the hob and place
the bowl of batter beside it.
4. Toss one-third of the scampi in the
flour, then drop them into the batter.
Scoop out and fry in the hot oil for
3–4 minutes, until the batter is golden
brown and puffed up. Drain on kitchen
paper. Prepare 2 more batches of scampi
in the same way and keep hot.
6. Serve with tartare sauce (see recipe 43).

95 **Hotpot**
[Serves 4]

– 900 g best end and middle neck British lamb
– 1 tablespoon groundnut oil
– butter
– 4 lamb's kidneys, skinned, cored and diced
– 3 onions, sliced
– 1 tablespoon plain flour
– 600 ml hot water
– ½ teaspoon Worcestershire sauce
– 1 fresh bay leaf
– 2 thyme sprigs
– 900 g potatoes, sliced
– sea salt and freshly ground black pepper

1. Trim the lamb of any excess
fat, cut the meat into chunks and
pat dry with kitchen paper.
2. Heat the oil and a small knob of
butter in a large frying pan until very
hot. Add the lamb, a little at a time, and
fry until brown, turning once. Transfer
the meat to a 3–4-litre casserole dish.
3. Fry the kidneys for a couple of minutes
until brown, then add to the lamb.
4. Fry the onions over a medium heat for
about 10 minutes, until soft and slightly
brown. (Use the same pan for all your
frying, adding more butter if necessary.)
Add the fried onions to the casserole.
5. Put the flour in the frying
pan, then gradually stir in the

water and Worcestershire sauce.
Keep stirring until smooth.

6. Season the liquid with salt and pepper
and bring to simmering point. Pour over
the mixture in the casserole dish.

7. Preheat the oven to
170°C/325° F/gas mark 3.

8. Add the bay leaf and thyme to
the meat, then arrange the potato
slices on top. Season and dot the
surface with a few dabs of butter.

9. Cover the casserole with a tight-fitting lid
and put in the oven for 90 minutes. About
15 minutes before the end of cooking
time, remove the lid and dot the surface
with a little more butter. Leave the lid off
and increase the heat to 200°C/400 F/gas
mark 6 for the rest of the cooking time.

100 Wild Boar Stew with Beer
[Serves 4]

– 1 kg wild boar meat, roughly chopped
– sea salt and freshly ground black pepper
– 3 tablespoons flour
– 2 tablespoons vegetable oil
– 250 g smoky bacon or lardons
– 1 onion, roughly chopped
– 2 garlic cloves, crushed
– 1 teaspoon fresh thyme leaves
– 4 juniper berries, crushed
– 1 teaspoon sun-dried tomato purée
– 500 ml strong ale
– 2 litres beef stock
– 2 or 3 wild boar sausages

1. Put the wild boar chunks in a bowl, add
seasoning and 2 tablespoons flour and
mix well. Heat half the oil in a heavy frying
pan and brown the pieces of boar a few
at a time. Transfer to a casserole dish

2. Fry the bacon, adding a little more oil
if necessary, and add to the casserole.

3. Heat the remaing tablespoon oil in
another pan and gently fry the onion, garlic
and thyme for 3–4 minutes until they begin
to colour. Add the remaining tablespoon
of flour and the tomato purée, and stir
well over a medium heat for 2–3 minutes.

4. Preheat the oven to 180°C/350°F/gas mark 4.

5. Gradually add the beer, stirring well,
then add the stock. Bring to the boil,

season and add to the casserole.

6. Cover and cook in the
oven for 90 minutes

7. Cut the sausages in half lengthways
and grill them for about 2–3 minutes
on each side until they start to brown.
Cut into chunks and add to the stew
for the last 30 minutes of cooking.

8. Check the boar to see if it is tender;
if not, return the casserole to the
oven for another 20–30 minutes.

9. Serve with mashed potatoes
and spiced red cabbage.

Recipes

101 **Haggis**
[Serves 4]

— 1 sheep's stomach, cleaned
  and scalded in boiling water
— heart, lungs and liver of 1 lamb
— 450 g beef or lamb trimmings, fat and lean
— 2 onions, finely chopped
— 225 g oatmeal
— 1 tablespoon sea salt
— 1 teaspoon freshly ground black pepper
— 1 teaspoon ground coriander
— 1 teaspoon mace
— 1 teaspoon nutmeg
— 1 teaspoon cayenne pepper

1. Turn the stomach inside out and leave
to soak overnight in cold salted water.
2. Wash the lungs, heart and liver. Place
in large pan of cold water with the
meat trimmings and bring to the boil.
Cook for about 2 hours. When cooked,
strain off the stock and set aside.
3. Mince the boiled meats, or get
the butcher to do it for you.
4. Put the mince in a bowl and add the
onions, oatmeal and all the seasonings.
Mix well and add enough of the reserved
stock to make a soft and crumbly mixture.
5. Spoon the mixture into the sheep's
stomach (still inside out), until it is just over
half full. Sew up the stomach with strong
thread and prick a couple of times so

that it does not explode while cooking.
6. Put the haggis in a pan with enough
boiling water to cover it. Simmer for
3 hours without a lid, adding more water
as necessary to keep the haggis covered.
7. To serve, cut open the haggis and
spoon out the filling. Serve with mashed
swede or yellow turnip, tatties (mashed
potato) and a Robert Burns poetry recital.

index

Index

235

Eat Britain! 101 Great British Tastes

Eat Britain! 101 Great British Tastes